*Consider the subtleness of the sea . . .
Consider them both the land and the sea*
—Herman Melville

Islesboro

LONG ISLAND

RESOLU

SEVEN HUNDRED ACRE ISLAND

JOB I.

Camden

LIME I.

LASELLE I.

Rockport

MARK I.

MAINE

Penobscot Bay

PORTLAND

Atlantic Ocean

BOSTON

NORTH HAV

VINAL

LITTLE DEER ISLE

BARRED IS.
BEACH I.
COLT HEAD I.
PICKERING I.
HORSE HEAD I.
GREAT SPRUCE HEAD
BARRED IS.
BUTTER I.
BRADBURY I.

Northwest Harbor
• Deer Isle

BEAR I.

FLING I.
EAGLE I.

• Sunset D E E R I S L E

SHEEPHEAD I.
Southwest Harbor

Stonington •

Deer Isle Thorofare
CROTCH I.

Merchant Row

ISLAND

ISLAND

0   1   2   3 MILES

Cutler

Double Beaches, Great Spruce Head Island

*Cease searching for the perfect shell, the whole
Inviolate form no tooth of time has cracked;
the alabaster armor still intact
From sand's erosion and the breaker's roll.*
—Alfred Tennyson

Summer Island

Hard Head Island

*Into every empty corner, into all forgotten things and nooks,
Nature struggles to pour life, pouring life into the dead, into
life itself. That immense, overwhelming, relentless, burning
ardency of Nature for the stir of life!*

—Henry Beston

"There was nothing anywhere that was unnecessary; nothing, whether the work of man or

Eagle Island

existed without a purpose."

Summer Island
Penobscot Country

by Eliot Porter
Edited by David Brower

SIERRA CLUB · BALLANTINE BOOKS

Acknowledgments

For their special help in making this book possible, I owe grateful acknowledgement to:

My wife, Aline, for her constant support and encouragement and sympathy;
Nancy Newhall, who devoted many months in an effort to interest publishers in this book years before the Sierra Club undertook its publication.

Mary Cable; Ellen Auerbach; Steve and Kathy Porter; Fairfield and John Porter, my brothers; my sister Nancy Straus and her husband Michael; my niece Anite Fuller; and Jimmy Schuyler, for reading the manuscript and for their valuable criticism and suggestions;

Eileen Mitchell and Russell D. Butcher, for their help with the quotations facing many of the photographs;

Kenneth Brower for reading and criticizing the manuscript, and Sidney J. P. Hollister for helping in revising it;

And especially I wish to thank David Brower and his wife Anne for their dedication to the highest standards in publication, for their faith in the book, and for their devotion in bringing about its publication.

E.P.

Sources

We are grateful to the following authors and publishers for quotations used within this book:

Bates, Marston. From *The Forest and the Sea* by Marston Bates. Copyright © 1960 by Marston Bates. Reprinted by permission of Random House, Inc.

Beston, Henry. From *The Outermost House* by Henry Beston. Copyright 1928, 1949, © 1956 by Henry Beston. Reprinted by permission of Holt, Rinehart and Winston, Inc.

Borland, Hal. "Grass" from *Sundial of the Seasons* by Hal Borland. Copyright © 1964 by the New York Times Company. Reprinted by permission of the New York Times Company and J. B. Lippincott Company.

Carson, Rachel. From *The Sense of Wonder* by Rachel Carson. Copyright © 1956 by Rachel L. Carson. Reprinted by permission of Harper & Row, Publishers.

Cather, Willa. From *O Pioneers!* by Willa Cather. Copyright 1913, 1941 by Willa Sibert Cather. Reprinted by permission of Houghton Mifflin Company.

Child, Charles. From *The Roots in the Rock* by Charles Child. Copyright © 1964 by Charles Child. Reprinted by permission of Atlantic Monthly Press, Little, Brown and Company.

H. D. (Hilda Doolitle). "The Garden" from *Collected Poems of H. D.* Copyright 1925, 1953 by Norman Holmes Pearson. Reprinted by permission of Norman Holmes Pearson.

Frost, Robert. "Neither Out Far Nor In Deep" from *The Complete Poems of Robert Frost*. Copyright 1936 by Robert Frost. Copyright © 1964 by Lesley Frost Ballantine. Reprinted by permission of Holt, Rinehart and Winston, Inc. and Laurence Pollinger Ltd. "Blueberries" from *Complete Poems of Robert Frost*. Copyright 1930, 1939 by Holt, Rinehart and Winston, Inc. Copyright © 1958 by Robert Frost. Copyright © 1968 by Lesley Frost Ballantine. Reprinted by permission of Holt, Rinehart and Winston, Inc. and Laurence Pollinger Ltd.

Jeffers, Robinson. "October Week-End" from *Such Counsels You Gave to Me and Other Poems* by Robinson Jeffers. Copyright © 1937 by Random House, Inc. Copyright © 1964 by Donnan Jeffers and Garth Jeffers. Reprinted by permission of Random House, Inc.

Jewett, Sarah Orne. From *The Country of the Pointed Firs and Other Stories* by Sarah Orne Jewett. Copyright 1896 by Sarah Orne Jewett. Reprinted by permission of Houghton Mifflin Company.

Lowell, Robert. "Soft Wood" from *For the Union Dead* by Robert Lowell. Copyright © 1963 by Robert Lwell. Reprinted by permission of Farrar, Straus & Giroux, Inc. and Faber & Faber Ltd.

Matthiessen, Peter. "The Atlantic Coast" from *The American Heritage Book of Natural Wonder*. Copyright © 1963 by American Heritage Publishing Co. Inc. Reprinted by permission of American Heritage Publishing Co. Inc.

Maxwell, Gavin. From *The Ring of Bright Water* by Gavin Maxwell. Copyright © 1960 by Gavin Maxwell. Reprinted by permission of E. P. Dutton & Company, Inc. and Longmans, Green & Co., Ltd. Anonymous Scottish Song from *The Rocks Remain* by Gavin Maxwell. Copyright © 1963 by Gavin Maxwell. Reprinted by permission of E. P. Dutton & Co., Inc. and Longmans, Green & Co., Ltd.

Pound, Ezra. "Provincia Deserta" from *Personae* by Ezra Pound, Copyright 1926, 1954 by Ezra Pound. Reprinted by Permission of New Directions Publishing Corp. and Faber & Faber Ltd.

Rich, Louise Dickinson. From *The Peninsula* by Louise Dickinson Rich. Copyright © 1958 by Louise Dickinson Rich. Reprinted by permission of J. B. Lippincott Company.

Scott, Winfield Townley. "Rose Island, For Roderick O'Connor" from *Change of Weather*. Doubleday & Co. Copyright © 1962, 1964 by Winfield Townley Scott. Reprinted by permission of Winfield Townley Scott.

Thomas, Dylan. "Poem in October" from *Collected Poems* by Dylan Thomas. Copyright 1946 by New Directions Publishing Corporation. Copyright 1953 by Dylan Thomas. Reprinted by permission of New Directions Publishing Corp. and J. M. Dent & Sons Ltd.

White, E. B. From *Stuart Little* by E. B. White. Copyright 1945 by E. B. White. Reprinted by permission of Harper & Row, Publishers, Inc. and Hamish Hamilton Ltd.

The Sierra Club, founded in 1892 by John Muir, invites participation in its program—a program that needs continuing and wide support—to preserve the nation's scenic and ecological resources, including its mountains, wetlands, wildlife, forests, wild shores, and rivers. Address: 530 Bush Street, San Francisco, California 94108.

Copyright © 1966 by the Sierra Club

All rights reserved. Published in the United States by Ballantine Books, a division of Random House, Inc., New York, and simultaneously in Canada by Ballantine Books of Canada, Ltd., Toronto, Canada.

Library of Congress Catalog Card Number: 66-20402

ISBN 0-345-25538-0-695

This edition published by arrangement with the Sierra Club, San Francisco

Manufactured in the United States of America

First Revised Printing: November 1976

Book design by David Brower

Birch and bridges, Great Spruce Head Island

Foreword

There are thick woods where sylvan forms abide...
—Percy B. Shelley

There was world enough then, and more time than there is now. Neither had to go and both can return. Not the times and the people whom Eliot Porter remembers here, for their time was a special one, a golden time, and they had room to live in it, room that let human spirit grow—the wide green land, the untroubled shore, a little alabaster here and there, and places no one thought to pave yet that are almost all slipping away now.

Whatever let it happen, Eliot Porter's world had something in common with Stuart Little's about which E. B. White wrote a paragraph that ought to be displayed in every town hall in the land. Because Mr. White knows Maine, we hoped he would introduce Eliot Porter's island world, but he couldn't. Nevertheless, his paragraph does.

"In the loveliest town of all, where the houses were white and high and the elm trees were green and higher than the houses, where the front yards were wide and pleasant and the back yards were bushy and worth finding out about, where the streets sloped down to the stream and the stream flowed quietly under the bridge, where the lawns ended in orchards and the orchards ended in the fields and the fields ended in pastures and the pastures climbed the hill and disappeared over the top toward the wonderful wide sky, in this the loveliest of all towns Stuart stopped to get a drink of sarsaparilla."

Stuart could still find sarsaparilla if he asked for it, but he would need something stronger were he now to look at what they've done to the edge of his town.

Whoever they are, those who did this to Stuart Little's habitat, we don't want them to do it any more, and we are sure they don't need to. Enough of the lovely towns have already lost their loveliness. It will add too little to the material development of this land, and take too much from its spirit, to diminish any more loveliness. Better to go back to the places man has lessened, to add evidence not of man's grossness or his neglect or his callousness, but rather of his genius. Let man heal the hurt places, and revere whatever is still miraculously pristine.

That is our biased aim, one we hope will be increasingly understood and widely shared. If it succeeds, there may be more time for sarsaparilla and less need for LSD. No one should underestimate the power of the reawakening that comes when time runs along at its own pace and not under forced draft, and there is a place to spend it in we want to know, or approach knowing, through what all our senses will tell us if instead of merely counting we learn to listen, or look, taste, touch, and see, or to comprehend.

Do something silly for a moment. Toss a precious object into the air and catch it. Now consider the extraordinary device (you, yourself) that just accomplished this everyday miracle. You sensed the energy of the toss, knew the value and the importance of success. You triangulated the position of the object throughout its flight with your binocular vision, you edited out distractions by other senses that might divert your attention, you brought an extraordinary signal mechanism into precise operation that triggered one set of muscles after another into a sequence of ground-to-air-missile direction-control processes resulting in easy success as you caught the object without thinking.

What you did will not make headlines anywhere. It is the simplest example I can think of of what you do millions of times a day. But ask your friends who know microelectronics best what it would cost, and how much space it would take, to achieve artificially what you just achieved naturally. He will admit that the problem of reconstituting these simple excellences of yours would require a major federal grant. But that's just for the easy part.

Remember that all the miraculous abilities you demonstrated can be naturally and automatically packaged, and preserved without the slightest impairment, for periods of twenty to fifty years or so, in an ultramicroscopic part of you, received by you at no cost and forwarded into the future at the same price, in a tiny segment of a gene in a chromosome in a solution so concentrated that a single teaspoon could contain all the instructions needed to build and operate the three billion people now on the planet.

All this comes free from nature, the nature too many of our best superficial minds think we can do without. We can't. We have already done too much of it in. There may yet be, in the untrammeled tenth of America, enough nature, unsecond-guessed by technological arrogance, to build a good future on. We must hope so, and treasure what we have. Not to make mass sandboxes out of, or Lake Powells, or highway and helicopter havens, but places where like Eliot Porter we perceive instead of just looking, where we listen a little and talk less, where we consider our beginnings and our beyondings, where we learn to absorb, and to respect and love and remember.

The wild places are where we began. When they end, so do we. We had better not speed their passing. Man's talent can keep them if he lets it.

Something happened and can still happen on a summer island to substantiate all this hypothesis. Drive near (you can't, happily, drive *to* places like this), park, and ask for a sarsaparilla, then think about the island and about the other places there ought to be that are like it enough to count, this year, next year, and forever after.

David Brower
Executive Director, Sierra Club

Trail on Pea Point, Great Spruce Head Island

Introduction

UNLIKE ELIOT PORTER, I came to a Maine island for the first time, not as a child, but as an adult—and in the winter, not in the summer. The island was Hog Island in Muscongus Bay. Little did I know then that it was to become a home, a base, and a springboard to hosts of other islands, and, I might add, an affair of the heart. I first saw Hog Island from the nearby mainland—out in the cold gray waters under a gray winter sky. Beyond it were islands and more islands, on into the open Atlantic.

This island, like most of the islands, was one of ineffable beauty. Spruce and balsam fir, in great mature forests, rose straight, tall, and limbless, their needled branches joining near their tops to form a green canopy. In the world of subdued light and silence below, the only sound was of waves on the shore. One walked noiselessly on the deep, soft carpet of needles, passing now and again outcropping rocks covered with lichens and mosses. Here one sensed a quality quite different from a mainland forest. Here one had the feeling of apartness, of aloneness, of being in a small, self-contained, finite world, at once insulated and bounded by the sea. This was the island feeling, a sense of wonder that I was to experience every time I visited a Maine island.

There are really two Maines. One is the vast interior mainland with its forests, lakes, mountains, and rivers. Along the 2,500 miles of coastline where that mainland meets the sea—in a multitude of harbors, bays, and peninsulas—the second Maine has been created, the Maine of sea-swept islands. There are hundreds and hundreds of them, from the smallest rock ledges barely exposed at high tide, to the great massive islands rising like fortresses out of the sea. And what a romantic history they have!

In 1524, Giovanni da Verrazano sailed up the New England coast as far as Maine admiring the lovely islands. "In fifty leagues," he wrote, "we discovered thirty-two islands, all near to the continent, small and of pleasing appearance, high, following the curving of the land, among which were formed most beautiful ports and channels, (as are formed in the Adriatic Gulf . . .)."

"We staid the longer in this place, not only because of our good harbor (which is an excellent comfort) but because every day we did more and more discover the pleasant fruitfulness; insomuch as many of our company wished themselves settled here, not expecting any further hopes, or better discovery to be made."

On Allan's Island there stands a granite cross bearing the simple and startling legend "Weymouth—1605-1905," a tercentenary commemorative marker placed there by a local historical society. On March 31, 1605, Captain George Weymouth sailed from England to explore the new world. His ship was the *Archangel* with 27 in crew. Fortunately for our history, among them was the scribe, Rosier, whose job it was to keep a written record of the voyage and all the places visited. From his faithful account, we have it that on May 11, the *Archangel* was off Cape Cod, Massachusetts. But Weymouth did not attempt a landing because of the shallow waters. Instead he proceeded on a northeasterly course, "Down East," as the saying goes. On March 17, he dropped anchor in the lee of a large island and went ashore, naming this island St. George after England's patron saint and himself. (Later the name reverted to the Indian name, Monhegan.) From the high bluffs, Weymouth's first sight of the new world he sought was a maze of islands against a backdrop of the rounded blue hills of the mainland.

But this labyrinthian complex of islands was no place to explore with a large sailing vessel. So Weymouth based the *Archangel* in the protected harbor between Allan and Benner islands in Muscongus Bay. From there, in a small pinnace, he explored the islands of the bay and the mainland by going up an incredibly beautiful river to where the town of Thomaston was later established. He named the river St. Georges, now the Georges. He and his men spent many days exploring the islands of Muscongus Bay and the Georges River. Three and a half centuries later I found that Rosier's detailed description of the plants and birds of the islands was still amazingly accurate.

In their primeval wildness, what a Garden of Eden those Maine islands were. The inner forested islands provided perfect nesting sites for bald eagles, ospreys, and ravens, for colonies of black-crowned and great blue herons. Up and down the coast on the outer islands, many of which were treeless, were great sea bird colonies—of herring, laughing, and black-backed gulls; of arctic, common, roseate, and least terns; of double-crested cormorants, eider ducks, black guillemots, puffins, and of the oceanic Leach's petrels. Captain John Smith, who maintained summer quarters on Monhegan Island in 1614 while he explored and mapped the coast from Penobscot Bay to Cape Cod, gave us an account of the bird life of the islands: "Eagles, Grives, diverse sorts of Haukes, Cranes, Geese, Brants, Cormorants, Ducks, Sheldrakes, Teale, Meawes, Guls, Turkies, Divedoppers, and many other sorts, whose names I knowe not." According to the intrepid Captain, a most trustworthy observer and chronicler, there was an Eden too in the sea surrounding the islands: "Whales, Grampus, Porkpisces, Turbot, Sturgion, Cod, Hake, Haddock, Cole, Cusk, or small Long, Shark, Mackerell, Herring, Mullet, Base, Pinacks, Cunners, Pearch, Eels, Crabs, Lobsters, Muskles, Wilkes, Oysters and diverse others."

The descriptions Captains Weymouth, Smith, and other early explorers left of the great spruce-covered islands, the treeless outer islands, and the waters of the innumerable bays and inlets conjure up a picture of a faunal and floral paradise—original communities of living things in all their primeval purity and beauty.

To be sure, the Indians used plants and animals for food, but such uses had little effect on the abundance. The Indians were nomadic by nature, their numbers relatively small, and their weapons crude, far less capable of total destruction than those of the more "advanced" white man.

As seems to be the lot of Gardens of Eden, the one here did not endure. It ended with the advent of the white man and his settlements. Most of the forested islands lost their trees to the shipyards, the home builders, and the box and barrel makers.

The eggs of sea birds were highly prized for food. On the outer islands, the great bird colonies were robbed of their eggs year in and year out without any thought of the law of supply and demand, and they dwindled almost to the vanishing point. Terns in particular were slaughtered unmercifully during the height of their nesting activities, and their skins shipped to the feather market in New York City.

Just last summer (1965), on Matinicus Island, an elderly lady surprisingly young for her ninety years, gave me a rare eyewitness account of the destructive nature of the feather trade in 1886. The victim was the arctic tern, one of the loveliest and most exciting species summering on the Maine coast. She recalled that a certain man would come each year from "away" (from outside of Maine) and would go to Matinicus Rock to kill the arctic terns that nested there by the thousands. Returning to Matinicus Island, he would unload barrels and barrels of the terns. Island women were hired to skin the birds and prepare their skins with preservatives for shipment to the mainland. She remembered the year 1886 in particular because she was eleven years old, the same age as the daughter of the man from "away." That was also the year that George Bird Grinnell, a sportsman, and owner and editor of *Forest and Stream*, alarmed by the awesome destruction of birds for plumage, founded an organization for the protection of birds and called it "The Audubon Society." (Although his society itself did not endure, it was the beginning of bird protection efforts that later became the Audubon movement.)

The tempo of these exploitations increased until the late nineteenth century. By 1900 there wasn't a tern left on most of the islands and most of the sea bird colonies were gone. Only farther Down East in the more remote Canadian Maritimes did the various birds find safe breeding grounds. So it took about three hundred years for this Garden of Eden to become a biological desert.

In the late 1890's and the early 1900's—just in time—the wildlife conservation movement began. It gave birth to the Audubon Societies and other preservation groups. Maine islands became the very first Audubon Sanctuaries. Beginning in 1901 the National Audubon Society engaged lighthouse keepers and other islanders to serve as wardens. As a consequence of broad-scale educational efforts, laws were passed giving protection to birds. The wild-bird

Osprey with fish, Great Spruce Head Island

Here too in Maine things bend to the wind forever.
—ROBERT LOWELL

plumage trade that became a "million dollar industry" was killed by public opinion and the law.

Slowly the islands were abandoned by their human inhabitants for the more comfortable and "civilized" living on the mainland. Over the years, the amazing succession of plant life that can produce a forest on bare rock, brought back the spruce and balsam forests to many of the islands. Protection brought the birds back to the outer islands. Today the nesting gulls, terns, cormorants, and eider ducks have virtually regained their earlier abundance, demonstrating the marvelous regenerative power that can, in time, remove even deep scars.

Whereas, in the past, economics and a desire for greater creature comforts have generally caused man to abandon the lonely and more difficult island living, now a vastly advanced technology makes it possible to travel and live almost anywhere, thereby threatening the wild beauty of these islands, as it threatens wilderness everywhere.

Fortunately, several islands have already been saved. The National Audubon Society maintains as sanctuaries Great Duck Island near Mount Desert; Ten Pound Island near Matinicus Island; Hog Island, the Todd Wildlife Sanctuary and home of the Audubon Camp of Maine, and Western Egg Rock in Muscongus Bay; and, with the help of Prouts Neck Audubon Society, Stratton and Bluffs islands. The Nature Conservancy preserves Turtle and Dram islands and is working toward acquiring others. And sensitive private owners have saved Great Spruce Head, the island that has inspired this book.

People who know the coast of Maine and those who have never seen it will cherish this book. Writing with the familiarity of one whose home has been a summer island, Eliot Porter evokes the very spirit and substance of the hauntingly beautiful coast. *Summer Island* is an eloquent plea, in words and in the author's inimitable photographs, to save the utter loveliness of those little microcosms of life—the golden isles of Maine.

CARL W. BUCHHEISTER, *President*
National Audubon Society

New York City
March 1, 1966

[17

Penobscot Bay, Southwest from Eagle Island

to my grandchildren

Contents

Foreword, 12

Introduction, 14

By Lunar Time, 21

Buying an Island, 23

The Hippocampus, 28

Exploring the Bay, 35

The Big House, 42

The Dragons, 48

Island Places, 55

Fog, 58

Matinicus Rock, 63

Becoming a Photographer, 72

Nests, 78

Voices in Spring, 86

Reunion, 90

Island Color, 96

    MORE LAND THAN SEA, 96

    THE BAY'S EDGE, 108

    IN WOODS AND MEADOWS, 117

    FOREST DETAIL, 124

    LIFE CYCLES, 137

    BY THE SEA WIND, 145

When your wares came from the seas,
  you satisfied many peoples;
      —Ezekiel 27:33

South from the Summit, Great Spruce Head Island

CHAPTER 1

By Lunar Time

TO A YOUNG CHILD reared far from the sea, as I was, our summer island was a reservoir of inexhaustible knowledge and adventure. In the tidal zone along the shores, the extravagant forms and adaptations of an abundant marine life served both to explain and to compound the mysteries of the sea; and the tides that ebbed and flowed on its shores were, and still are, a source of never-ending wonder.

The day of my first visit to Great Spruce Head Island was what people like to call a typical Maine summer day. The sky was a clear, deep blue. Penobscot Bay, mirroring the sky, was a darker blue, here and there ruffled into an even deeper hue by gentle breezes that left between their erratic efforts pale streaks of calm water.

The image of the Island that forms most clearly in my mind when I remember that first trip, is a sweep of white beach, a dark mass of forest behind it, and in front of it, holding the beach to its arc, a lobe of pure translucent blue.

This is not to say that I am unable to recall many events or circumstances of the comings and goings and doings of the large family to which I belonged. These are well placed in my memory. But the mental picture that one paints of a place is a different kind of memory, its ingredients including many faint and ill-defined experiences that went unrecognized when they happened. The constant batter of impressions adds piece by piece to the substance of memory built up in many dimensions, of which time and place are less important than sensations and emotions.

So I also retain a few other memories of that first day. I walked with my aunt to the hilltop that is the highest point on the Island to survey the Island's extent. Our appearance there surprised a herd of wild cattle pastured on the hill's slopes by island farmers. They galloped off in a whirlwind of alarm over rocks and brakes and fern until they had gained the safety of the farthest shore. The Island then was more barren and open than it is today, having been overgrazed and repeatedly cut over for wood. A spruce forest now completely covers that hill and most of the then open lower land as well, so that the general impression has changed from one of rock and grass and slopes of hay-scented fern, of open views and easy accessibility, to one of dark forests, more confined vistas, and impenetrable thickets. It is hard now to believe how open the island was.

Everything else that I remember of the Island comes from the half-century that passed from that first year, in 1912 when I was ten years old, when my father bought it as a place to take his family in the summer.

Our lives there, my brothers' and sister's and mine, were from the first determined by the sea. High tide was the time to swim; and low tide the time to explore the shore. We set our clocks ahead before daylight-saving time had been devised in order to enjoy the daylight hours more fully. We gathered shells along the high-tide wrack: powder blue and purple mussels in all sizes that nested together in compact families; pale green sea urchins washed clean of their spines; and the perfectly preserved, brilliant orange carapaces shed by the small, brown-green crabs that live in the rock weed of the littoral zone. We collected starfish, sunstars, and sand dollars, and dried them under the kitchen stove. From the shallow edge of the sea, we dredged up anemones, sea-cucumbers, limpets, and coral-like calcareous algae. Our father explained the names and relationships of all these creatures to us, and took an even greater interest than we in this ever-present museum of marine biology.

So it was that we began to live by lunar time. A deep feeling for nature began to grow in me, a feeling that was to affect the whole future course of my life.

Penobscot Bay, North from Peak Island

CHAPTER 2

Buying an Island

IN THE COURSE of his search for a suitable summer place in the East, my father visited friends at a marine biological laboratory in Casco Bay. Delighted by the rough, irregular Maine coast with its fringe of innumerable islands, and by the northern climate, he decided then that an island was what he wanted. As he journeyed farther north along the coast to Penobscot Bay, he became more and more captivated by the wild beauty of the country. He inquired about islands for sale and explored many of them; but he could not find one that satisfied him. Then, one day, from the wharf on Islesborough, he saw among a group of islands four miles out in the bay, one island higher than the others. He asked about it, found it on a chart, and immediately wired the owners an offer. He then hired a boat to take him to it. It far surpassed his hopes. It was small enough to be an island to children, yet large and varied enough to promise constant enjoyment. Shortly thereafter we owned Great Spruce Head.

Part of our enjoyment of the Island came from unraveling its history and tracing it as far into the past as possible. In post-Revolutionary War times, when the mainland was still largely unsettled, our Island, like many islands along the Maine coast, was inhabited by fishermen-farmers. Because we know little about them, we reconstruct their way of life by projecting recent history back to their times. They probably got about in slow broadbeamed sailboats like the later Friendship sloops, a far cry from the graceful yawls and sloops of today. They also rowed themselves from island to island on shorter journeys.

From the caved-in cellar holes lined with field stones that survive today on many of the small, long-unoccupied islands, we know that the islanders' homes were solid and roomy. Were they made of logs chinked with pitch and sphagnum moss or of hand-hewn planks and timbers? We don't know, for all other evidence has been completely effaced by the erosion of time. We do know, however, that these early dwellings were not the precise work of ship carpenters, who, a century ago, built the white, ship-lap, colonial cottages of retired sea captains, cottages now greatly admired up and down the New England coast. The island houses were crude, and were weathered to the gray of their doorstep stones and the barnyard walls.

Many islanders lived their whole lives on the islands where they were born; there they died and there they were buried. To survive, they had to be self-reliant, to build their own boats, to raise all the food they did not take from the sea, to attend to their own sick, and to treat their own injuries. Doctors were few and far away, and there were no hospitals. Women must have often borne their children alone, and surely saw many of them die in infancy.

On Great Spruce Head Island there is a small graveyard surrounded by a wide wall made of stones removed from the cultivated fields. The wall was probably intended to keep out the trees and undergrowth, but it has not succeeded. Trees are crowding in from all sides. Under the low, spreading branches, held tightly among the roots and half-buried in the sod, lie six stained and weathered white marble slabs commemorating those who died on the Island. On one is carved the name, "PHOEBE, WIFE OF THOMAS P. HASKELL, DIED AGE 25." She was a Walton and she probably died in childbirth. Two graves, side by side, bear legends for Mr. Paul Walton and his wife, Abigail, who died within six days of one another at the ages of 84 and 77. And on another slab the eroded letters simply say, "JOHN WALTON, DIED IN APRIL, 1805, AGE 105." Who was John Walton? No sure record exists. His genealogy is lost in the unrecorded, forgotten past. He was not born on the Island, that much we know, but went there from the mainland. Was he perhaps the founder of the Walton farm that occupied the southern half of Great Spruce Head Island? Was he indeed born in 1700? Or had he, in his declining years, forgotten his own birth date?

During the early part of the nineteenth century, the Island was divided between two families. The Parsons, about whom we know even less than about the Waltons, lived at the north end, where the cellar of their house has survived to this day. That the two families did not get along well and may have quarreled over land is suggested by the remains of a cedar fence that once divided the Island across its low midland. For our first ten years on the

Island we could still trace this fence from the head of the Cove through the boggy woods to the west shore. The line was made by moss-covered fallen logs whose spiral grain clearly indicated that they had once been cedar posts. Now all trace of them has disappeared.

As land travel improved during the late nineteenth century and coastwise ship travel increased, the coastal settlements in Maine slowly grew. Clusters of homes around the shore of Penobscot Bay became villages and then towns. Of all these towns, the most engaging today, and in many ways the most attractive, is Stonington. It is situated at the southern end of Deer Isle, the large island that forms the eastern boundary of the bay. The painter, John Marin, made Stonington his summer home and there painted many of his famous watercolors of the Maine coast. Stonington, unlike the other bayshore towns, is the only one that has had a long history of fishing and quarrying. While the shipyards and lime kilns were prospering in Rockland, and Camden was becoming a base for yachtsmen, the Crotch Island quarry opposite Stonington was shipping granite by coasting schooner to New York City. There it was used in the construction of Grand Central Terminal and in many of the parkway bridges in Westchester County and neighboring Connecticut. For more than a generation, Crotch Island has produced a uniform, fine-grained granite, and now the island is half cut away. The derricks rising above the quarry are a landmark for the ships passing through Merchant Row between Deer Isle and Isle Au Haut to the south, or through the narrower Deer Isle Thoroughfare, which winds among the many islands that lie off Deer Isle's southern shore.

Since the town of Stonington is built along the shore of a shallow tidal cove that opens onto Deer Isle Thoroughfare, its houses come right down to the water's edge, where many of them are supported by piling. Those behind this waterfront row stand in tiers on a granite hill, their foundations exposed above the ground, their cellars quarried out of solid rock. Although granite quarrying is its major industry, Stonington is a wooden town, granite having been used conspicuously only in the construction of retaining walls and in the largest piers. Consequently, as you approach the town by boat it presents a façade of white, cream, and yellow buildings and of gabled roofs rising back in echelon from a frontage of wharves. The monotony of clapboard fronts is relieved only by the irregularly spaced dark rectangles of many mullioned windows. The first line of buildings faces inward on the principal street, which follows closely the curve of the shore. Many of the houses on the bay side of that street are built on piles and serve both as shops and as dwellings. At the backs of those in which fishermen live, rough plank wharves are used to store lobster traps. They are piled in neat rows with coils of warp and colored buoys packed inside. Each fisherman has his own bright color combination for his marker buoys, which, when not in use, are kept freshly painted and stacked behind his house or hung from the walls of his paint shed. Every lobsterman has his own dock, whether behind his house or away on a piece of land on the harbor shore. To it he brings his boat at high tide, and there he has his workshed for building and maintaining his string of traps.

Lobstering is the second major occupation of the natives of Stonington. Lobsters the fishermen sell to wholesalers in Stonington find their way into all the retail markets on the eastern seaboard. Dozens of lobster boats are moored in the shallow cove, and every dry ledge and tiny islet is taken over as a repository for the new and worn-out gear of lobstering. To keep the mess away from the house, warp and nets are usually tarred on these islets, the black tar spilling in streaks over the orange granite. But lobstering is not the only kind of fishing carried on from Stonington. On the town's largest wharf, a sardine factory cans the herring brought in by seiners from all along the coast, and by local fishermen when they catch more than they can use for lobster bait.

Herring seining, if one listens to those who make their living by it, is an uncertain business, dependent on the vagaries of the fish and the whims of their buyers. Fate seems to conspire against the seiner, who with a typical New England pessimism always takes a gloomy view of his prospects. When herring are plentiful, the price is too low to make seining profitable; when they are scarce, even the high price they demand does not cover the costs of catching them. But for some inexplicable reason, the seiner keeps on fishing. Sometimes, when a plentiful catch drops the bottom out of the market, the seiner can make his venture pay by selling herring scales for the manufacture of artificial pearl buttons.

Stonington, because at first I felt a stark and desolate atmosphere there, seemed to me to be a town displaced from its proper environment. It was not a New England town; it belonged in the far north. Its angular, graceless houses

Houses, Stonington

These houses made the most of their seaward view, and there was a gayety and determined floweriness in their bits of garden ground; the small-paned high windows in the peaks of their steep gables were like knowing eyes that watched the harbor and the far sea-line beyond, or looked northward all along the shore and its background of spruces and balsam firs. When one really knows a village like this and its surroundings, it is like becoming acquainted with a single person. The process of falling in love at first sight is as final as it is swift in such a case, but the growth of true friendship may be a lifelong affair.

—Sarah Orne Jewett

were more suitable to a gold-camp community or an Alaskan frontier town near the Arctic Circle. But this was no more than a superficial judgment, for when Stonington is seen from its streets rather than from outside its harbor, it is a friendly town. From the inside, so to speak, Stonington's character becomes warm and cozy, even in the sharp light of a hazeless day. This quality derives as much from the closeness of the houses as from the gay flower gardens that each householder manages to bring into luxuriant bloom on the smallest plot of thin soil.

Dahlias, a Stonington favorite, do well in the cool Maine climate; and geraniums, pansies, and petunias also thrive beyond expectation. Flowers complement the handiwork of the lobstermen. While he paints his pot buoys in vibrant colors behind his house, his wife cultivates a bright garden beside her doorstep. The buoys blossom on the surging sea around the kelp ledges, marking the traps that reap a rich harvest from the bottom of the ocean; the flowers, a harvest of the land, blossom from the decomposing granite, which gives its mineral richness to the soil.

Lobsterman's house, Stonington

CHAPTER 3

The Hippocampus

ON THE MAINLAND one can at least always walk to his destination. But the islander, unless he is willing to live under the most primitive pioneering conditions, needs a boat. To get about between the islands and to the mainland for supplies, the first island settlers depended on wind and sail or rowed in dories. Even during our first summers in Maine, a few fishermen still rowed in a day the twelve miles to Camden on the mainland, and then back. Occasionally, on a calm day, we would see one of them in his dory, standing face forward as was the custom, rowing in an even rhythm by leaning against the oars. By pivoting on his feet like an inverted pendulum, the weight of his body literally falling against the oars, he could row the high-sided dory almost tirelessly all day long, attending to his lobster traps or setting his trawls for halibut and cod. Nowadays, with fish scarce and the gasoline engine a common source of power, fishermen lay their traps and set their trawls over a wider area and farther out to sea. They work now from fast high-powered motorboats equipped with sonar and radiotelephones.

Before the days of railroads it was more convenient to travel by water than by the highways on land, so the islands were settled first. Automobiles and super-highways, however, have so changed things that today all but the bigger islands are largely deserted, and the smaller ones are becoming the sites for summer homes of out-of-state owners.

While our house was being built on the Island, father also ordered a custom-made motorboat with sleeping accommodations for eight people. He named it the *Hippocampus*, Greek for "seahorse," or, more literally, "horse monster." At the beginning of that first summer in 1913, as in many succeeding summers, we traveled to Maine from Boston on the Bangor boat, disembarking in the early morning at Rockland. The Eastern Steamship Lines operated a coastwise service from Boston to Bangor, with two ships, the *Camden* and the *Belfast,* sailing on alternate days throughout the summer. The ships, more like river or lake excursion steamers than ocean-going vessels, were not built for heavy weather, being of shallow draft in order to negotiate the Penobscot River. They were thus forced to put in to Portsmouth or Portland harbor when overtaken by severe storms. Except for their black funnels, they were all white. Two narrow decks, onto which the outside cabins opened, encircled them from bow to stern and were surmounted by the lifeboat deck, from which the pilothouse stuck up like the cabin on a tugboat. Near the water line on both sides amidships, below the passenger decks, wide cargo ports opened for the freight that was wheeled onto the boat by hand. To push the trucks up the steep incline of the wharf slips at low tide was a labor that sometimes required the combined efforts of several stevedores.

Departure time from Boston was late in the afternoon. As we embarked at the Eastern Steamship Pier on Atlantic Avenue, we left behind, at once, the odor of roasting coffee and city grime, and began to enjoy the evocative harbor smells of fresh paint, tar, sour hawsers, and salt water. From that moment, we knew we were in a new environment—that of the sea. We stayed on deck in failing light as the boat passed down Boston Harbor and through the outer islands into Massachusetts Bay. If the weather was clear, we could see the lights of Lynn and Marblehead to the north. Perhaps we would even wait for those of Cape Ann, marking the northern end of the bay, before we went below to the dining saloon for a fish supper, and then on to bed. Connection with the interisland steamers that plied the waters of Penobscot Bay was made at Rockland, the first stop on the schedule, at four in the morning. Several of these smaller steamers, miniatures of the Boston boats, ran on daily schedules, stopping at settled islands and towns along the mainland. During those first years, one of these steamers, the *Catherine*, touched a mile from Great Spruce Head at Butter Island, where a summer colony thrived until the war. Not a house, and hardly a foundation, remains there today to tell of that once prospering community. To be sure that Rockland passengers would rise in time to get off, a porter would knock on their stateroom doors at the unconscionable hour of 3 A.M. If this warning were omitted, the likelihood was remote indeed that any passenger would sleep through the racket

28]

and clatter of donkey engines during docking, or the subsequent thumping and trundling of the freight being unloaded. And if the passage from Boston had been foggy, as in June it often was, the blaring of the foghorn at three-minute intervals through the night would have kept him awake anyway. The early hour or the weather, though, never seemed to matter; for with the dawn just breaking on the first day in Maine after a long winter, there was no staying in your bunk.

I remember that during that first summer we did not take the *Catherine* but were met in Rockland by Captain Monte Green and the *Hippocampus*. For me, and I suppose it must have been so also for my sister and brothers, that occasion was a fairyland experience. I had hardly been on a boat before, and never one like that. The polished brass, bright varnish, and compact cabin, the ropes and helm and winch and anchor, and all the rest of the nautical paraphernalia were new, exciting, and unbelievable.

As children do, we learned very quickly about boats, the conventions of navigation, and nautical terms. We soon knew the names of all the rigs of all the coastwise sailing vessels and ocean-going ships. We learned to row and even to scull as the native Mainers do, feathering our oars on the backstroke by dropping the wrist. We soon mastered all the pilot rules, and the kinds, colors, and names of buoys. We knew what nuns, cans, and spars were, and the difference between channel and reef markers. We learned that you leave a red buoy to starboard on entering a harbor, remembered by the three R rule: red, right, return. We learned to splice rope and to tie all the useful knots. And we learned the idiosyncrasies of the tides and the positions of the unmarked ledges in our vicinity.

At the end of the first summer, Captain Green promised to make us each a toy sailboat during the winter months. He did not describe what kind of boats he was planning to make, but told us only that we would be able to take them out in our rowboats and race them in the harbor. My imagination supplied all that was left unsaid. I dreamed about that boat throughout the school year; in retrospect it seems scarcely ever to have been out of my mind. This might have been the build-up for a heartbreaking disappointment, but because I had never owned a toy sailboat and so could not visualize what one would be like, the boats far exceeded anything I had conceived of in my wildest dreams. I was overwhelmed by them. In the first place, they were much bigger than anything I had imagined—over two feet long. They were two-masted racing schooners painted white and green, with full sets of white cotton sails. We loved them and immediately set to work to name them. My younger brother came up with the only original name; he called his the *Biddy*. My sister ostentatiously named hers *Medusa* and named mine the *Nautilus*. These models were soon serving the double purpose of decoration and toy, for when we weren't using them they were ensconced in cradles on the balcony railings at the ends of the living room.

After we had spent four summers on Great Spruce Head Island, the United States became involved in World War I. As part of the war hysteria there were frequent rumors of German submarines off the New England coast, so father loaned the *Hippocampus* to the navy for antisubmarine patrol. At the same time, Captain Green enlisted in the Coast Guard. The *Hippocampus*, with a crew of four or five seamen, was assigned to his command, but first she was completely remodeled to make her more seaworthy for patrol in heavy winter seas. For stability, a ton of concrete was poured into her hold, and for greater effectiveness against enemy ships, a wireless was installed and a machine gun mounted on her bow. Although the *Hippocampus* never was in combat, she did help to rescue fishing boats in distress in the rough winter seas and occasionally was sent on missions to carry sick and injured islanders to the mainland for medical care.

With the end of hostilities in 1918, the *Hippocampus* was decommissioned and hauled into drydock in the Charleston, Massachusetts, Navy Yard. Delays in renovating her for civilian use finally provoked father to ask that the *Hippocampus* be returned to him in Maine. The government, eager to be rid of the boat, launched her immediately—with her seacocks open—and she sank into the Boston Harbor mud. The navy wanted to declare her a total loss and pay a token compensation, but father insisted that she be raised and towed to the Island, despite her crippled condition. During the following winter, the *Hippocampus* was rebuilt, with a bridge amidships, a galley forward, and a large aftercockpit—but without sleeping quarters. For many years thereafter, we used her for day excursions in Penobscot Bay, but never again for overnight cruises. The concrete is still in her hold.

Another story that circulated around the bay in World War I arose because of our status as newcomers to the region. Newcomers anywhere, and especially in New England, are looked upon with suspicion in times of anxiety and crisis. It was not too surprising, then, that the "rusticators" (a colloquialism for summer residents) on Great Spruce Head were rumored to be German spies, who by means of their boat were in communication with enemy submarines. This opinion was fortified by a concrete tennis court that father had built in a clearing in the woods soon after our first summer on the Island. Tennis, a game

City Hall, Stonington

Wharf, Stonington

at which father was very good, was not as well known then among the islanders as it is today. The large slab of concrete was a structure they could understand only in terms of their experience and their wartime suspicions, which naturally suggested an obvious relationship. In their minds, the tennis court became a secret gun emplacement to be used against the United States when the opportune time arrived.

Monte Green, whom we called Captain Green, was more than a yacht skipper; he was also the caretaker of Great Spruce Head, where he lived the year around with his wife and three small children. During the winter, he chopped wood for the Big House and for his own use and cut the ice and stored it. In the spring, he planted the vegetable garden and painted and launched the *Hippocampus,* which spent the winter in the boathouse on the Island. A native of Penobscot Bay, he knew every island, ledge, and harbor in it, and a great deal, too, about the whole Maine coast. Everyone knew and liked Monte Green. His relationships with children, who, including us, adored him, grew out of a boyish, playful, and perhaps somewhat irresponsible quality that he possessed to a highly refined degree. With easy unselfconsciousness he knew what children liked to do because he liked to do the same things himself. Owing to years spent on the water, he had developed a peculiar squint that compressed his eyelids into a triangular shape. To me, this squint was the *sine qua non* of a Maine boatman and I tried in vain to imitate it.

Captain Green lived with his family down near the wharf and boathouse in a small house that he had built himself with material father supplied. It was probably in comparison with this house that from the beginning the cottage (the native term for all summer houses) we lived in was always referred to as the Big House. When Captain Green enlisted in the Coast Guard, father hired Lewis Shepard, an elderly farmer from Little Deer Isle, as caretaker. He lived with his wife and a son about my age in the house Captain Green had built. Since Mr. Shepard's duties consisted only of haying, woodcutting, and taking care of the vegetable garden and the buildings, and did not include maintenance of the boats, the house in which he lived came to be known as the Farmhouse.

To our great disappointment, when the war ended Captain Green did not return to us. He had obtained a more lucrative position elsewhere. From then on, for a number of years, a series of boatmen of varying competence worked for us. None stayed very long until two brothers from Eagle Island named Erland and Bonny Quinn took charge. They could do anything that had to do with boats, and they knew the bay as well as Captain Green did. About this time, Lewis Shepard retired and a young, taciturn fisherman named Rupert Howard, also from Eagle Island, applied for the job of caretaker. He was a strong, self-confident man and father hired him. Rupert turned out to be not so taciturn or distant as he had at first appeared. His observations on nature and people, and especially on us and our activities, were always to the point and entertaining. We were constantly quoting what he said and laughing at the humorous and kindly fun he poked at us. Soon we were on first name terms with the Howards, which was never the case with the Shepards, with whom it was always Mr. and Mrs. We became so fond of Rupert and Lottie Howard that when they left, after twenty-five years, it was like the breaking up of a family. Rupert kept the buildings and equipment in perfect repair, and the garden always flourished under his care, owing as much to his innate feeling for growing things as to the absence of drought during those years. He always had time, too, for all the extra work that we asked him to do during the winter months.

During our first years on the Island, the plowing and hauling was done by a horse. When the Shepards came, however, we bought an ox, because Mr. Shepard, an old-world farmer from Nova Scotia, knew the art of driving oxen. The ox, whose name was Dyke, could draw a wagon or pull a plow in his slow, swaying gait. Mr. Shepard did the mowing by hand with a scythe. Fascinated, we would watch him tirelessly swing his arms and body together, stroke after stroke, as he advanced around the meadow a step at a time. Periodically, he would stop and whet his scythe with a long stone, like a carver at Thanksgiving preparing to attack the turkey. The rasping ring of stone on steel, which could be heard for a great distance, told us that Mr. Shepard was at the mowing long before we came upon him in some remote corner of the meadow. The ox, unfortunately, died on the beach after licking clean a can of paint accidentally left within his reach.

Dyke was replaced by an aging horse named Prince, whose teeth—the surest indicator of a horse's health—we failed to inspect before we purchased him. In a few years he became too feeble to work and was replaced by a caterpillar tractor. Rupert was very soft-hearted and would not dispose of Prince, allowing him the run of the Island all summer and only occasionally, when he could be caught, hitching him up for light work. The haying then was done by tractor and the hay stored for Prince and the cows during the winter. For several years, when Rupert kept no cows on the Island during the winter, the hay was still cut for Prince. Finally, however, he became so weak that he had to be shot. Because Prince was his friend and trusted him, Rupert refused to perform the execution and hired a neighboring islander to do it.

Before the Howards came, the white clapboard barn was built in the field above the harbor beach near the Farmhouse. It had a large hayloft and stalls for four cows and a horse, though no more than two of the cow stalls were ever occupied. Rupert brought his own cows to the Island and we bought milk from him. When the Howards came to the Island, father built a new farmhouse for them in the same style as the barn. The old house, which was much smaller and completely inadequate in comparison with the new one, was converted into a chicken house, and there Lottie kept the hens whose eggs she sold us.

When Rupert retired, a period of bad times began. One caretaker followed another in quick succession; few stayed more than a year and each one departed leaving the buildings and equipment in disrepair. They could not bear the loneliness and isolation of the winter months nor do the routine work that was required. Those who remained longest had been reared on islands and understood the exigencies of island life. The job of a caretaker on a Maine island is a demanding one in many ways. It requires a more than ordinary sense of responsibility, a great self-reliance, a philosophical acceptance of prolonged isolation, and a love of island life that is only possible for those who have grown up from childhood on the islands. The Shepards and the Howards had this background; their successors did not. They did not make needed repairs in time, either not seeing the necessity for making them promptly, or lacking the will to get them done. They cannot be blamed; they simply were not equipped, physically or psychologically, for this kind of responsibility. During this period, the wharf was damaged in a storm, the boathouse doors blew off, the electric plant failed and was not repaired, the tractor broke down, the house went unpainted, insufficient wood was cut, and the garden was planted too late.

At last, a few years ago, my youngest brother found a young man who combined in his temperament and skills all the attributes a caretaker must have. He had grown up on a neighboring island and preferred island life to life on the mainland. He was responsible and conscientious. And he was skilled in many trades: in carpentry, in mechanics, in boatbuilding, in farming, and in the lore of fishing and the sea. He accepted the position of caretaker and moved to the Island with his wife and children. Since he took over, the establishment on Great Spruce Head Island has been maintained in impeccable condition. This man is Walter Shepard, the grandson of Lewis Shepard, who was in charge of the Island a generation ago. He belongs to a breed of men rare today, men who seek from life what few desire—room to maneuver and breathe freely on the sidelines of a high-pressure civilization. His independence is in the best tradition of island people, shaped as they are by their association with the sea.

There's sometimes a good hearty tree growin' right out of the bare rock, out o' some crack that just holds the roots; right on the pitch o' them bare stony hills where you can't seem to see a wheel-barrowful o' good earth in a place, but that tree'll keep a green top in the driest summer. You lay your ear down to the ground an' you'll hear a little stream runnin'. Every such tree has got its own livin' spring; there's folks made to match 'em.

—SARAH ORNE JEWETT

Great Black-backed Gull with young

CHAPTER 4

Exploring the Bay

UNDER the guidance of Captain Green we explored Penobscot Bay. He introduced us to many of its islands, tidal inlets, and rocky, surf-pounded outer shores. Instinctively, he knew the places that offered children and adults alike adventure and the excitement of exploration. He took us on excursions to nearby land-locked basins, like miniature inland seas. These were accessible only at high tide and only through the narrow passages into which the Captain skillfully piloted the *Hippocampus* or rowed us in the tender. When the tide was high, the water in these granite basins came up almost to the lower branches of the spruce trees that grew precariously in the cracks and hollows of the rounded rock. On sunny days, this basin water was often as warm as that of a fresh-water pond, perfect for swimming before a picnic lunch.

The Captain also showed us the bird islands on which gulls and terns nested in dense but separate colonies. The Spoon Islands, named for their inverted spoonlike profile, were down the bay on the outer side of Isle au Haut, and being the most distant, were the most exciting of the bird islands to visit. Barren, treeless heaps of rock exposed to the Atlantic swell, these two islands, Great Spoon and Little Spoon, were to me a world apart—an unbelievable, isolated place, in a limited way, complete in itself.

Ever since I can remember, birds have fascinated me. By the time we started going to Maine, I knew most of the common birds of northern Illinois, where I was born, and felt that of them the most mysterious, because so seldom seen, were the bitterns and rails of the prairie marshes. But I had never seen a bird colony until I visited the colonies of gulls in Maine. As had happened when I discovered a nest of buffy bittern eggs in Illinois, these gull colonies stirred in me excitement and wonder; in both I recognized an other-worldness beauty undisturbed by human trespass.

As we approached the boulder-strewn shore of Great Spoon Island that served as a beach, alarm spread among the birds. They rose in screaming clouds, wings flashing against the blue sky like scraps of paper blown upwards by a puff of wind. Against their unanimous clamour, their din of cries at the invading humans, one could hear the voices of single birds—the low-pitched, bugling calls of swooping gulls and the piercing, staccato cries of the terns, racing by on stiff, beating wings close above us.

Early in the summer most of the gull's nests contained eggs. In a few the eggs were pipped, and some contained still-damp, just-hatched young. Later, when the gray-speckled, downy chicks were all out, the nests would be empty and the chicks would be found with their heads buried, ostrichlike, in the grass or with their bodies wedged in crevices in the gray lichened rocks, relying instinctively on protective coloring and frozen stillness to escape detection. On these islands, however, gulls are by and large safe against predation, having no enemies except a few ravens and, paradoxically, their own species. Young gulls removed from their hiding places will run off when released in panicked search of new concealment, which they may find in the territory of another pair of adults. If they do, they are in danger of attack by the established residents, who may peck them to death before they are able to reach the safety of their own nests. Terns are more vulnerable because of their smaller size. Their principal enemies are the gulls, who destroy large numbers of young terns when the colonies of the two birds are close together. Gulls, ever watchful for the opportunity, swoop down on unattended tern nests, devouring both eggs and young. Ordinarily, this is not a great hazard as terns and gulls usually colonize separate islands, the terns selecting the small grassy islets where gulls would be too crowded.

Young Herring Gull

Herring Gull's nest

One year, at the instigation of Captain Green, we brought home two young gulls as pets. Since they could not be distinguished from one another, we named them Tweedledum and Tweedledee. Raising them was an easy task, for they quickly adapted to us as foster parents. They were also omnivorous and could be fed on anything from table scraps and fish cleanings to clams and mussels, even eating sea urchins and starfish when all else was unavailable. They grew prodigiously, waxing fat under our care. When their baby down was replaced by feathers, they were released from their pen and allowed to roam free. Everyone approaching the Big House by the trail from the dock was greeted by Tweedledum and Tweedledee, begging insistently for food. Far heavier than the wild gulls, and lacking the example of other young birds and the competitive stimulation of colonial life, our pets were slow in learning to fly. Eventually, however, instinct and genetics won out over a comfortable dependence. After much wing flapping and running up and down the path to gain momentum, they gradually succeeded in taking off—at first in short, clumsy flights, but at last in longer flights down over the bank to the water. The process was like a recapitulation of the development of the airplane. These first flights, however, were only the beginning of their final emancipation; for weeks they continued to return to the house to be fed. But the reversion to the wild was inevitable. Soon they stopped coming to our front door, being content to beg for food on the beach and at the dock. Long after they had ceased to depend on our care, they would come when we whistled, fearlessly, and sometimes accompanied by a cautious wild bird who, through their example, dared to risk, for handouts, the perils of human beings. Yet, even after they had left for good, we knew them from their wild companions by their size, strength, and aggressiveness.

Often during our excursions in the *Hippocampus* we entered charted but unbuoyed waters thick with reefs and ledges. Even with government charts to guide us, navigating required both familiarity and skill, for which we depended on our captain. His knowledge of the obscure nooks and crannies of the Maine coast seemed almost unlimited and was in truth the result of years devoted to poking about the islands and harbors, both out of curiosity and in search of livelihood. He piloted us through tight passages, with a swell running high on the ebb tide, and came so close aboard to reefs that we could look down through the foamy water to the streaming brown weed and feel the power of the sea surging over the rounded, seaweed-covered backs of submerged rocks. Like monsters they were, roaring and rearing their mossy heads in a lather of foam and spray as though waiting their chance to destroy us; and all around them in the green, turbulent water, the dim, waving outlines of kelp aprons gave ominous warning. The names sea captains and fishermen gave long ago to these ledges reveal the fears they could inspire at night, or perhaps the imputation of some animistic power. Thus we find on the charts of the coast such names as "The Brown Cow," "The Washers," and "Roaring Bull Ledge." There are stories, too, which add to the malignant reputation of the sea along this rugged coast, stories of disasters occurring in the dead of stormy winter. Ships and crews have disappeared and left only a half-obliterated name on a fragment of splintered driftwood wreckage.

One rugged island was so difficult to land on that we seldom visited it—but always enthusiastically. Seal Island, fifteen miles to seaward from the entrance of Penobscot Bay, is a last rampart of land, with the whole width of the Atlantic stretching beyond. It is a treeless ridge of granite on which, in pockets of peaty soil, a curious vegetation has become established. Besides grasses and morning glories, various kinds of sedum thrive in the salty atmosphere, and a variety of prostrate juniper not found on any of the other inshore islands hugs the flat rocks in a close mesh of interlacing stems. A trip to Seal Island should only be made when the weather is propitious in all respects. First, there should be no fog, which means waiting for the condition that usually follows a period of northwest winds that drive any lingering fog banks well off shore. A day that starts with a glassy bay and a clear sky, but with a white band of haze barely obscuring the southern horizon—the kind of day that promises to be warm—is a day to avoid. That faint white blending of sea and sky, easily overlooked because it seems to bode no ill, is a sign of inclement conditions. It usually indicates offshore fog that will come rolling in as the prevailing southerly afternoon breezes spring up, if not far up the bay at least to cover the outer islands. Another condition to be avoided, because it effectively prevents landing on Seal Island, is a heavy ocean swell following stormy weather. The only landing place in any weather is on the relatively sheltered bay side of the island. Only once were we able to land there in moderate surf, and that was because some lobster fishermen, camped on the island for the summer, brought us ashore on a shelving rock in their flat-bottomed dories. Our round-bottomed rowboat might have been smashed had we attempted it, whereas a dory could ride the waves up on a shelving ledge to be caught and held as the water receded and we scrambled out.

The outer side of Seal Island, its chief attraction, is sheer cliffs, in many places fifty or more feet high. Against these, the ocean swells crash, throwing spray high over the island. The power of the surf is almost unbelievable and is manifest in a slow-motion action that gives no indication at first of the energy involved. No shallow water borders this exposed side so the waves do not break before striking the cliffs. Instead, they draw back and rise against them slowly, noiselessly, as though they would gently lap the face of the rock. Suddenly, just before the wave peak reaches the cliffs, something happens to the calm coherence of the wave. It spreads into a massive sheet of blue-green water that climbs up the face of the rock, disintegrates, and widens into a fan of white spray and foam that crashes down on land and sea. At one place, where an eroded lava dyke has left a wide, deep crevass extending down its whole face, waves funnel in and squirt geyserlike up the slot to twice the height of the cliff. Fishermen christened the slot Squeaker Guzzel.

But excursions in the *Hippocampus* and rowboat trips to the nearby bird islands were not the only boating adventures we had on Penobscot Bay. A year or two after our first summer in Maine, father bought a small speedboat in Boston that he named the *Squid*. By the standards of today it was not very fast, having a top speed of twenty miles an hour. But then it was like the wind compared with the speed of a fishing boat powered by a two-cycle engine. The *Squid* was V-bottomed with an engine under a hatch that covered the forward half. It had a windshield and a driver's seat just aft of the hatch, a steering wheel like an automobile's that gave the boat a glamorous appearance of power, and a cockpit behind the driver with seats on either side for passengers. On a glass-calm surface the *Squid* was fun to drive, but on waves it pounded badly, and even in a moderate sea had to be slowed way down to avoid nosing under. In these conditions it wallowed slowly along, much less seaworthy than an equally slow fisherman's boat.

The *Squid* was shipped to Maine on board the Bangor boat and at Rockland was transferred to the steamer *Catherine*, which brought her out to Butter Island. In her crate, the *Squid* was a fairly large piece of freight and delayed the unloading of other cargo at Rockland. For the little *Catherine* she was almost too big to be carried at all and could only be loaded crosswise so that she projected through the cargo ports on either side. The difficulties of transferring the *Squid* from one steamer to the other delayed the departure of the *Catherine* for several hours. The passengers who were eager to get to their destinations became more and more restive and angry with each added delay.

My whole family was waiting on the dock at Butter Island to see the new boat arrive. We had been waiting a long time without suspecting what had caused the *Catherine* to be so late when at last she was spotted coming up the bay with what looked like an enormous bone in her mouth. Then we knew. But the *Catherine's* troubles had just begun, for it proved much more difficult to extract the crated *Squid* from the steamer's bowels than it had been to put her there. There were more delays, consultations between the officers, and advice from shore. Various abortive attempts were made to get the crate out. Meanwhile, the passengers began to express their uncomplimentary opinions of the person responsible. The captain got mad. To avoid identification with the situation, father and mother withdrew discreetly to watch the unloading struggles from a distance. Father told us children to keep quiet and not to say a word about whose boat it was. None of this bothered us a bit. We thought it was a momentous occasion and enjoyed it all. In the end the *Squid* was disgorged without too much damage by being uncrated. The climax came when she was suspended over a widening gap between the wharf and the steamer—her bow on one and her stern on the other—as the *Catherine* slid off sideways. When she splashed into the water, the passengers, I am sure, and probably the crew as well, hoped she would sink. It would have saved the day for them if she had, but they were disappointed.

For father, the *Squid* was mostly a toy in which he enjoyed taking his friends for short rides around the Island. On one of these trips he hit a submerged rock while traveling at full speed. Fortunately, only the shaft and propeller were damaged and he managed to limp home. After that he seldom took the *Squid* out, but, rather surprisingly, allowed me to use her often. I took her all over the bay, sometimes in heavier weather than was wise.

The most exciting trip I made in her, however, was after the war while I was still in college. My roommate was coming to visit me from Mt. Desert Island and was traveling by way of a steamer that stopped at North Haven in the evening on its way back to Rockland. It was a calm day, but there were thunderstorms about. I went down the bay to meet my guest in the late afternoon, taking the shortest route by going through the passage called the Little Thoroughfare. It is a rather tricky route, full of ledges and small islands, but safe at any tide if you know the course, and I was sure I did.

The steamer from Mt. Desert, a sidewheeler named the *J. T. Morse*, was late so that we started for home in the dark. Several thunderstorms had moved into our part of the bay; soon rain began to fall, at first lightly and then in sheets. Although there was no wind, the rain was driven hard against the windshield by our speed. Because it was impossible to see through the windshield, I steered standing up, looking over the top with the rain beating in my face. Frequent flashes of lightning illuminated the islands and

> We were standing where there was a fine view of the harbor and its long stretches of shore all covered by the great army of the pointed firs, darkly cloaked and standing as if they waited to embark. As we looked far seaward among the outer islands, the trees seemed to march seaward still, going steadily over the heights and down to the water's edge.
>
> —Sarah Orne Jewett

sea around us and guided me on the course. With each flash, we were thrown from almost complete darkness into dazzling light. During these flashes we saw a silvery bay in the distance and dark water close at hand, pock-marked by the rain that was coming straight down. There was a slight swell, which in those instants of vision gave the polished surface of the sea a molded, wavy appearance. All around, the silhouettes of rocks and islands stood out clearly. I steered past these known landmarks at full speed, exhilarated during the periods of darkness by not knowing when the next flash would come and I could again reset my course. We twisted through the Little Thoroughfare and out among the islands at its entrance, picking up one by one the ledges and buoys by which I knew the passage. We came out into the more open bay and headed for Great Spruce Head. The lightning flashes continued to light our way intermittently; the rain never let up. When we were within two miles of home we saw a light that at first I could not place. It was where no light should have been and yet seemed to be where we were going. And then I realized that someone had placed a lantern on the dock to guide us—my father.

Boat house, Great Spruce Head Island

CHAPTER 5

The Big House

ONE OF MY earliest impressions of life on the Island is of a steady stream of visiting friends and relations. Seldom was the Big House not full. Both my parents were instinctively very generous, always eager to share their pleasures with their friends. But it was mother whose warm personality attracted a large circle of friends and who cultivated a full and rich social life for herself and her family. Father had inherited from his mother a shy aloofness that was a handicap to him in establishing rapport. This social disadvantage was partly offset by my mother's support and by a material generosity that perhaps even exceeded hers.

Our family was a close-knit one in which we children shared more than ordinarily in the intellectual life of our parents and their friends. As a result, we grew up feeling very much a part of adult society and at home in it. We were never pushed aside or left out of discussions if we showed any interest in them, but we were also taught respect for our elders and not treated with the undue deference that in later years became a popular way to bring up children.

We were also encouraged, as we grew into our teens, to have our own friends visit us. They were often invited for much more extended stays than the adult visitors. Fairbank Carpenter from Chicago was my best boyhood friend and spent several summers with me, becoming very much one of the family. Adults were invited by my mother for shorter and more definite periods of time, for a week or perhaps two. But visitors there always were and our table was often full, even though it seated as many as twenty, or twenty-two with a little crowding.

Smooth management of the providing of food and preparing of meals is a matter children always take for granted. I see it in retrospect as a tour de force worthy of almost unlimited admiration, and an accomplishment due as much to the skill of our very competent Swedish cook as to my mother's efficient planning. There was always plenty of food, consumed by the children with as much speed and gusto as good manners, dictated from the ends of the table, would allow. The more than enough food for everyone at mealtimes was, of course, not enough for the children, for our strenuous activities in, on, and out of the sea created a hunger that was insatiable. In spite of the despairing protestations of Josephine the cook, we devoured unrecorded quantities of doughnuts, leftover pie, and raisin bread. One item of food was free for the taking at all times: bananas. A full bunch of them was kept hanging on the kitchen porch and it became a reflex to grab one as we dashed through the kitchen and down the back steps.

Fairbank proved to be a highly skilled kitchen diplomat, establishing with Josephine a friendly and valuable relationship that enabled him to be au courant about the leftovers in the pantry. Although I frequently had to use dissimulation to get around our cook, my friend rarely needed such a technique. His charm won Josephine's favor and gained for him, and indirectly for me, many special considerations. Once, at the end of our noon meal, he asked if he might have a doughnut and was told by mother that they were all gone. He permanently established his reputation for inside knowledge about pantry inventory by pointing out that there were still one and a half left in the bread box.

Summer table manners were often less formal than those we had been taught in Winnetka. With new guests we followed the convention, when we were not served by the maid, of passing plates from person to person along either side of the table. The main course was served by father at the head of the table and the dessert by mother at its foot. The twelve-foot table built of two-inch-thick cypress was oiled and waxed to a high gloss. Mother never used a tablecloth so the dishes slid easily on the polished surface. With old guests, or as geniality gradually eased the formality between ourselves and new guests, father would often scoot the filled plates down the table instead of passing them. He became skillful at giving just enough of a shove for the distance the plate had to go, and we all helped to intercept plates that were inadvertantly pushed too hard. When someone wanted a dish passed, he would ask the person nearest to it to give it a shove in his direction, and it would come sliding across. Of course, there were accidents— glasses of milk would get spilled or other dishes upset— but the custom was never abandoned on that account.

At the noon meal, with the dessert, a large box of candy was often passed around. Father had a sweet tooth and frequently during the summer he bought five-pound Whitman's Sampler boxes. Guests brought us candy, too, so there was almost always a supply on hand. No sampling—no "spit-backs"—and no lingering over choices or digging into a bottom layer were the rules. If one of us children took too long, the others would call out, "No fair!" Our motto was, "One swift glance and select the largest." This system worked very well, except when the box contained chocolate-coated marshmallows, which, though big, none of us liked. Nougats and caramels were our favorites. Sometimes, when good friends were visiting who had not yet been fooled, and in spite of mother's disapproval, father would place in the box as a decoy a smooth, chocolate-colored piece of jasper that he had found on the beach and that looked just like a big nougat. As the box was passed around, we all waited for the unsuspecting guest to follow our example of picking the largest piece, and so fall into the trap. No one ever broke a tooth on the stone as mother feared someone might; but many were chagrined by the greediness that the deception revealed.

The big table had rails connecting the corner legs at such a height that the temptation to put our feet on them and tip back in our chairs was almost irresistible. Until we were grown up, however, mother never allowed us this pleasure, and whenever we succumbed to the temptation would order us to sit up straight and stop tipping. The adults, though, often sat that way during conversation around the table when the meal was over.

Among my parents' friends who visited us for several weeks one summer were two marine biologists from Boston. They had been invited to make the Island their headquarters during a marine invertebrate collecting expedition to Penobscot Bay. Because of his own interest in the project, father put the *Squid* at their disposal for dredging purposes. Every morning, weather permitting, they would set out with Captain Green for the deepest places in the upper bay and spend hours dragging back and forth at slow speed. They had a small drag like those used for catching scollops but with a net of finer mesh. Every twenty minutes or so it was raised and emptied of whatever had been scooped up. Only once was I allowed to go on one of these dredging trips, but I still remember the fascination with which I watched the dumping of the dredge into buckets in the stern of the boat. All sorts of new and strange marine animals were brought up. There were various species of mollusks whose shells we never found on the beaches—delicate, pink, calcareous, fanlike things suggesting a tropical sea—varieties of echinoderms and crustaceans whose names I can only guess at today, and once, unbelievably, a small octopus. These creatures were sorted out and embalmed in jars of alcohol, all of the most interesting specimens going to the gentlemen from Boston. Father did keep some of the surplus, however, storing the specimens on a shelf in his room until, some years later, the alcohol had all evaporated through the seals on the jars.

One of the biologists had been in Harvard with father and was an old friend of my parents. When it was too rough to go dredging in the bay, he would go out alone at low tide to collect specimens along the shoreline. Not once did he return from such forays in time for meals. Mother was very good-natured about it, accepting his tardiness as an inevitable consequence of his preoccupation, but she and father were amused that every time he came back he offered a different excuse, as though he had been aware of his lateness and was prepared with an apology.

Certainly the life on the bottom of the bay was more exciting and mysterious to me than the cultivated vegetables and wild fruits that grew abundantly on the Island. Yet, because those vegetables and fruits were almost always on our summer dinner table, I gained from them a kind of direct and sensuous knowledge of nature's variety that I have never forgotten. In our own garden we grew peas, beans, lettuce, carrots, beets, spinach, chard, corn, and potatoes. In late summer we also gathered several varieties of wild mushrooms. But of the Island's wild edible foods, its berries are its greatest gift. Sun-ripened and sweetened in the salty air, they have no comparable rivals among cultivated commercial varieties.

All the usual kinds grow in their characteristic habitats: raspberries favor the shrubby, impoverished sides of the pasture—the clearings where firewood has been cut—and flourish in dense tangles over the fallen trunks of blowdowns; blackberries prefer the damp edges of the alder bogs where they intertwine their head-high, scratchy stems and establish barriers that only the most intrepid pickers attempt to penetrate; blueberries, that most typical of New England wild fruit, mat the stony pasture slopes. And in peaty soil on headlands above the bay when the air is crisp with a foretaste of fall, one finds the slow-ripening highland cranberries that can be cooked into a more tangy, tart, delicious sauce than the Cape Cod cranberry has ever made. Intermingling with the heathery crowberry, the cranberry bushes form a closely woven, springy mat, which smooths over all lesser irregularities of the rough ground. Upon arriving at such a place, the picker is tempted to forget the berries, to stretch out in the heathy, sour fragrance and the relaxing warmth of the sun, and give up

[43]

Lasell Island

Rain-water pool, Seal Island

all purpose, surrendering to the indulgence of his senses. Who says that to dream away an afternoon with a foam-streaked bay spread out before your half-shut eyes and a wind stroking your face is not as purifying as gathering a small basket of bullet-hard berries for cranberry jelly?

None of the berries, however, can equal the wild strawberries in flavor and sweetness. They come in June and early July and are found in their most luscious size deep in the meadow grass. Mother was an indefatigable berry picker, and the strawberries, being first, were the ones she most enjoyed gathering. Her favorite beds were in the South Meadow, from where she could look down the sloping grass to the Indian shell heaps above the beach, to the dotted rocks and small islands beyond, and on out to the open sea. This meadow had a history of redmen's feasts, of canoes drawn up into the grass and blazing campfires, and later, of a white man's farm and his small sailboat anchored off shore. Mother often thought of the Indian women who in their time had gathered berries in sweetgrass baskets like her own. She expressed her feelings in a poem she wrote in 1919.

She spent many hours in the meadow, stooping beside a patch of strawberries and carefully hulling each berry she picked. Finally, she would return with a basket full of rich, red, juicy fruit, clean and ready to eat. Never would she accept from other pickers unhulled berries for household use because they involved too much work for someone else to prepare.

Her lovingly gathered troves were made into desserts for the whole family. If the harvest had been especially large, it was converted into strawberry shortcake the like of which defies description. The foundation of this remarkable production was not a doughy biscuit but a shortbread worthy of the fruit it supported, and whose juices it soaked up. If the harvest was not large enough for shortcake, the berries were made into a deep pink, smooth, creamy ice cream, the freezing of which became the responsibility and not unpleasant duty of my brothers and myself. The reward was always licking the dasher, so there was never a shortage of volunteers, even though the bounty had to be shared between us.

Strawberry ice cream was not the only kind made; other fruits were used and at times such ingredients as chocolate and caramel. Ice cream was a Sunday custom, the only event that distinguished that day from the rest of the week. On Sunday morning, we would haul ice from the ice house, wash it, and shave it. Then, when the freezer was filled, we would sit on the back porch steps and turn the crank. After many summers, we got to know exactly how many turns were needed for each kind of ice cream and wrote this information down on the screen door jamb. Raspberry ice cream, I remember, took the most turns.

STRAWBERRY PICKERS IN PENOBSCOT BAY

I question and wonder as the gulls go flashing
Over rocky meadows stretching to the sea,
What women long since silent gathered these red berries,
Who were those came questing ages before me?

Did the bronzed squaws leave their warriors sleeping,
After the feasting by the shell-heaps on the shore,
To wander here and search among the boulders,
Staining their fingers with this same crimson store?

Did the later harvesters of long-ago summers
Listen to the white-throat who sings unweary still?—
They who after toil at the sea and the ploughing
Now lie so quiet in the graveyard on the hill.

Ghosts of the gleaners from Alder-swamp and hillside
Come thronging to companion my quest and my mood
When the pail overflowing with June's fragrant berries
Makes glad the homing to the nest that holds my brood.

Butter Island beach

CHAPTER 6

The Dragons

MY LOVE for Great Spruce Head Island and the pleasure it has given me are in large measure derived from the education in natural history casually and unconsciously passed on to me by my father. In spirit, he was a naturalist. His father, who was an Episcopal minister, died when he was five. His mother, a very shy and devout woman, became more and more of a recluse after the deaths of her husband and an older son, eventually going into a deep mourning that she maintained for the rest of her ninety years of life. She attended church regularly until she became too feeble to go out and always said grace before meals, a custom that awed and amused but did not arouse reverence in her grandchildren. My father grew up when Darwinism and mechanism were gaining their greatest triumphs over fundamentalism. His mother's religious beliefs and religious teachings, to which he was subjected in his youth, were insufficiently convincing against the logic of the evolutionist. To the credit of my grandmother's liberality, she accepted her son's scientific modernism without protest. But through the ethical teachings of early childhood, on which the influence of the science of his day was later impressed, my father developed a way of thinking—a scientific integrity of mind—that led to inevitable conclusions. Of these, the most important was a rejection of the theological dogmas concerning the origin of the physical and living worlds—and man's place in them—for a world without design or purpose. Consistent with his childhood training, however, he retained an extreme sense of moral responsibility. This feeling was particularly noticeable in his attitude toward my brothers and sister and me. He believed that since parents were solely responsible for the existence of their children they had an inescapable responsibility for the happiness and moral integrity of those children. Such a view left out of consideration the genetic phenomena as well as the environmental and social forces that mold the individual. But those omissions did little to weaken the effect of the viewpoint. In fact, it was one of the determining factors in my father's decision to buy an island. In his boyhood, my father formed with some young friends the Agassiz Club, an organization for scientific discussion that survived until its members were dispersed by the requirements of higher education. My father continued to pursue his interests in natural history throughout his college career. Biology, especially marine biology, was his chief interest, although he studied geology and astronomy intensively enough to become conversant in both. He kept up with the current theory in these subjects so that later he was able to pass on to us ideas and information that colored our educational background.

Among the earliest pleasures I remember before we started going to Maine for the summer were the walks we took with father along the beaches of Lake Michigan. He always had much information to impart to us, not didactically, but spontaneously in the course of ordinary conversation. He was constantly in search of mineral specimens or on the lookout for interesting natural phenomena, and always shared with us his knowledge of the things he found and saw or answered the many questions we asked. We hunted for fossils and learned about crinoids, trilobites, and amonites. We found geodes lined with beautifully refractive quartz crystals and were told the theories on the formation of the earth's crust. We learned about meteors, stars, and the origin of our planet. Once, in an argument after school, I asserted that the moon was much smaller than the earth. For this statement I was unanimously ridiculed by the other boys, but I remember that I remained defiant with my superior knowledge.

That life on the Island was a consummate joy was attested to by our despair and my sister's tears at the end of that first summer. We lived together in one big house, the house my father staked out the first time I visited the Island. The large central living room, rising two stories to the roof, was flanked on either side by covered porches. On the southern-facing one, at the enormous table the builder of the house had given to father, we ate our meals in all weather. From either end of the living room, the house continued into two stories of small rooms, the kitchen at one end with bedrooms above, and bedrooms on both floors at the other end. The upstairs rooms were reached by staircases that led to balconies. Four rooms with a central bathroom occupied each floor at each end. Beyond the bedrooms at both ends, the house ended in sleeping porches. On the ground floor off the kitchen, however, the porch served the practical needs of household management. There were located the icebox, set tubs, ice cream freezer, vegetable racks, and other utilities. On the same floor with the kitchen were bedrooms for the cook and the maid. The four rooms on the second floor above the kitchen were always reserved for guests.

The other end of the house, to the east, was the family end. My parents occupied the two rooms on the second floor that opened onto the porch, where we children often slept. On foggy mornings, we would wake to find our canvas covers drenched and our hair and pillows wet with droplets of fog. On such mornings, a goodly measure of character or adult persuasion was needed to pry us out of the warm comfort of our beds into the damp, chill air and into equally damp clothes. My room opened onto the balcony and faced south across Penobscot Bay; my next younger brother's room, also opening onto the balcony, was across the hall. Three of the downstairs rooms were assigned to my sister and two youngest brothers; the fourth was reserved for our more intimate guests.

A huge brick fireplace capable of accommodating four-foot logs extended across most of the kitchen end of the living room. Above the mantle hung a plaster cast of one of the Elgin marbles from the Parthenon. The woodwork was stained dark brown and the beaverboard walls were painted chrome yellow. The floor, after a few years of a sticky oil finish, was scraped and painted oxblood red. The walls of the living room were decorated with an oriental rug, an embroidered Chinese dragon, India prints, and Egyptian bedspreads. The bedspreads, which were of hideous geometrical, appliqué design, were gifts to father that he either could not bear to discard or was afraid to discard for fear of offending the donors. Norwegian gargoyles, Japanese paper fish, and a ceramic plaque of sea horses, the emblem of father's first boat, completed the decor of the room. This heterogeneous and garish decoration had come about not as the result of any plan but through a process of slow accretion. For us children, who grew up under its influence, so to speak, the display was simply a part of the house. We accepted it uncritically and even took a certain degree of pride in it, a pride reduced only from time to time by the politely restrained, unenthusiastic comments of visitors. My mother, I believe, was more conscious of the room's atmosphere than the rest of us, for she once remarked that she felt as though she were living in a medium's parlor.

The final embellishment of the room was the result of father's passion for dragons. It was the product of a labor that lasted many weeks one fall, when mother was away on a visit and father was left alone in the Winnetka house. During those weeks, he spent all his spare time in the unventilated attic, painting panels to fit the sloped ceiling of the Island house living room, and at the same time nearly ruining his health by breathing the fumes of the Duco enamel he used. What he created were very boldly designed dragons in the most flamboyant colors obtainable. When the panels were installed the next summer, the dragons dominated the living room, stretching for thirty feet along its whole length. A violet, green, and yellow beast, the male of the species, with huge red batlike wings, occupied one side. On the opposite wall, a wingless female, equally garish, hissed at two young dragons, one of each sex, sporting on her tail. There was no denying the spectacular quality of this creation. The dragons became famous. They were always shown to visitors, and many people—good friends and even casual acquaintances—stopped off on their cruises to see them. But the dragons also created contention in the family, which eventually became divided in its judgment of them.

Fairfield, one of my younger brothers and a painter, eventually inherited the Big House. I had never heard him comment on the dragons until one evening a few years ago. We were talking in front of his fire, as in the past, when the subject of the house and the room we were sitting in came up. He told me that he did not like the dragons, that they dominated the room and were too much like something out of *The Wizard of Oz*. He would like to remove them, he said, but hesitated for fear of offending other members of the family. I immediately backed him up—the house was solely his to furnish as he chose—and offered to remove the dragons for him, since he did not want to take the responsibility himself. I know he was glad of my support, and when I went to get a ladder while we were still in the mood, we both experienced the conspiratorial excitement of the occasion. When the panels were down at last, the room assumed a much more peaceful and quiet atmosphere. But this was not the end of the matter; the family became sharply divided on the removal of the dragons, and even some of our friends took part in the controversy. One of those friends rented the Big House from Fairfield the next summer and insisted that she would not go through with the rental unless the dragons were put back. So back they went; they have remained up ever since.

Our evening activities, whether reading, playing games, or conversation, always centered around the fireplace. Hardly a summer evening passed when we did not burn an armful of spruce cordwood that was cut on the Island dur-

Boats on beach, from Pickering Island

Spruce woods, Fish Hawk Point, Great Spruce Head Island

ing the winter. The abundant supply of this wood has never diminished, and even today, with five houses to provide for, the stove and fireplace consumption does not keep up with the growth of the forest.

Reading was our most common evening activity. Not only did we read to ourselves, but much of the time mother would read aloud to us. She was an indefatigable and swift reader, and could go on for hours. She had so highly developed the art of reading aloud that, as she herself sometimes admitted, she could continue automatically and without evident break for moments at a time after she had actually fallen asleep. In any case, she read to all of us, individually and together, until we were grown up—and to father, too. When we were young, of course, the books she read were for children: *Rewards and Fairies, Treasure Island,* and the *King Arthur Tales.* As we grew older, she read many novels, both classical and current fiction. After supper, when darkness had settled over the Island, we would build up the fire, light the kerosene lamps, and curl up on sofas—those who got there first. Then, while watching the shifting tongues of flame stroke the sooty bricks, we would be carried away into the world of Jane Austen, Thomas Hardy, or the latest novelist, or perhaps into the excitement of a mystery story.

Sometimes our evenings were varied with music from an ancient Victor Gramophone with a large flaring horn as depicted in "His Master's Voice" advertisements. Father had a fairly large collection of operatic and vocal recordings that he often played for his guests on the windup turntable with cactus needles. He had many Neapolitan songs, as well as duets from the classical operas sung by Tito Schipa, Antonio Scotti, Geraldine Farrar, Enrico Caruso, Emilio de Gogorza, and many others. When he turned on the machine, even with the inadequate recordings and weak amplification, Caruso's powerful voice would echo through the room, enhanced in volume and resonance by the acoustics of the high ceiling. The lilting, carefree tune of "La Donna è Mobile" from *Rigoletto* and the sentimental "A la Luz de la Luna," or "Linda Mia," particularly stick in my mind. But "Mamma Mia Che Vo' Sapé" sung by Caruso was the most popular and, for me, the most emotion-laden of them all. Most of these records, still preserved in remarkably good condition at the Big House, have the power to transport me forty years or more into the past. I can even hear the crackling of burning logs through the music as the atmosphere of those long-past evenings comes rushing back.

Often, on those summer evenings, the music continued after I had been sent off to bed. Lying there, I would listen through the thin beaverboard wall to the slightly muffled and softened tunes, truly enraptured until lulled finally to sleep.

Compared with contemporary standards of comforts and conveniences—what in our present-day, civilized technology have come to be regarded as necessities—life on the Island was in some respects austere. For light at night we depended on candles and kerosene lamps. Why these venerable means of providing illumination for the interior of a house should now be regarded as unsatisfactory I do not know. They served us very well for many years until father, in a moment of modernizing enthusiasm, was persuaded to buy a Fairbanks Morse electric light plant. Before its introduction, only our age determined how late we could sit up if we happened to be engrossed in a book. With the advent of modern power, however, instead of finding ourselves liberated from the exigencies of primitive ways, we found ourselves, surprisingly, less free. It is true that the lights were brighter and the shadows in the corners less dark, but the light was no better where it was needed, namely, on the page of a book. When it came to sitting up late, we were told that by doing so we were running the batteries down and that perhaps it would be more considerate and more foresighted to go to bed. Father's final argument, based on his having replaced the gasoline water pump with an electric motor, was that if the batteries became discharged we would be without water as well as without light, and that then we would be in difficulties. Partly to avoid this dire consequence of too profligate a use of electricity, though there never was a real danger of running the batteries down, father would start the generator in the evening. It was a noisy affair, and we were all glad when he turned it off, even though that was a not very subtle signal to retire. But since he would never trust anyone else to shut it off, when he did so, it was a matter of either being off to bed or sitting up under the cloud of his mild disapproval.

Before the modern days of electricity, our water supply was obtained from a drilled well with the aid of a two-cycle gasoline engine. So abundant was our supply during those pre-World War I days that all our guests were greatly impressed, reasonably assuming that fresh water on such an island would surely be hand pumped and hauled. In fact, though, the water was delivered by the pump to a pressure tank, from which it was forced into the house whenever it was required. The tank was so large that it was necessary to run the pump only once a day. The speed of the engine that drove the suction pump was controlled by a governor and a large fly-wheel. It ran with what seemed to be an erratic and halting rhythm, chugging away for a few strokes, then lapsing into silence, except for the whirring of gears that were carried along by the inertia of the fly-wheel. When the speed fell to a point at which the governor no longer shorted out the ignition, it would cough out an explosion or two and coast along again. From a distance, the sound was almost indistinguishable from the song of the black-billed cuckoo that inhabited the Island alder thickets.

Although cold water was constantly supplied to all the bathrooms, the hot water situation was quite different. At the kitchen end of the house, water was heated by the cooking stove, so our guests, who occupied the rooms above, usually found hot water available to them in limited supply by the end of the day. At the family end, on the other hand, hot water was provided by a separate heater. Down in the foundations under the sleeping porches, a small room had been blasted out of the rock and a hot-water tank and old-fashioned coal stove installed. To obtain sufficient hot water for baths, the stove had to be stoked up well in advance. In addition, because the draft was a tricky operation, constant attention had to be given to it to avoid getting only lukewarm water or, at the risk of an explosion, a boiling tank-full.

Preparing hot water for bathing was not often undertaken for the benefit of the children. They kept their bodies clean, though salty, by swimming in the ocean, a perfectly adequate method, as those adults who are hardy enough to swim in water at 55 degrees will testify. Children usually don't mind cold water—that is, water not confined to a bathtub—nearly so much as adults and will stay in for much longer periods of time.

One cold-water bathing custom that prevailed from time to time was begun by one of our most popular guests, an old friend and camping companion of father's. So instinctively and sympathetically did this man respond to the enthusiasms and hero-worship propensities of young boys that he could induce them to take part with doglike obedience in almost any activity he proposed. During his first summer stay on the Island, he announced that an early morning dip before breakfast was the most healthy and invigorating way to start the day. He quickly persuaded my younger brother and me to join him in this swim, which soon became a ritual. Once we had committed ourselves, my brother and I both knew that no defection would be permitted. We never really wanted to get out of the swim, but now and again, just to test our hero's determination, we would pretend to refuse to join him. Thus, after the swim itself had become established, another part of the ritual was for us to remain in bed after he had summoned us. Up and ready to go, he would shout from the center of the living room, "All ashore who's going ashore." When we didn't appear promptly, he would come up to our rooms and rout us out of bed, a reaction we had hoped for and had awaited with tingling excitement. The more we resisted; the more determinedly he played the game, which invariably ended in our being turned out, bedclothes awry, beyond any possibility of return. We would then, at last, adoringly submit and, with our towels and clothes over our arms, follow him to the beach. At high tide, with the water up on the steep, gravelly part of the beach, we could get in and out quickly, and the swim was actually pleasant. But with the tide out, the rocky shore covered with barnacles and sea urchins, and a long, shallow stretch of water to wade through, it was more than an ordeal, even in our sneakers. Regardless of the circumstances, however, our tyrannical hero would splash in without hesitation, setting an example that we could not fail to follow.

Our meals at the big table on the porch were often shivery affairs, especially breakfast or supper during stormy and foggy weather. Breakfast was served not long after sunrise, partly because we liked to rise early to make the most of the daytime, but also because we lived by our own daylight-saving time. We set our clocks two hours ahead during the first summers, and then, later, only one hour ahead as a compromise with the climate and our guests' conventional habits.

Following a day and night of southeasterly winds blowing in out of the Bay of Maine, fog would rest thickly over the Island. The porch screen at breakfast would be filled with thousands of tiny, glistening, liquid lenses; wet wisps of fog would drift down the length of the porch; and the big table, set for the first meal, would shine with condensation. On such mornings, hot cereal and coffee for the grown-ups were as absolutely essential as were warm sweaters. Only the bravest or most ostentatious would attempt to sit through breakfast under these conditions without extra clothing. Beside the door between the porch and the living room hung a thermometer and an aneroid barometer. Every morning father would tap and reset the barometer and announce the temperature to the guests. When the weather was particularly bad, he always did this, it seemed, with a certain gleeful satisfaction in the extremes of the Maine climate. Perhaps he felt that the temperature would somehow lessen the discomfort of anyone with enough appreciation to enjoy meteorological inclemencies. Occasionally, we were kept inside the house at mealtime by one of the most extreme of those inclemencies —a northeast storm that drove gusts of rain onto the porch. But even on those rare days, we felt that our surrender to nature was a display of unpardonable weakness.

[53

Grass and rocks, on Fish Hawk Point

CHAPTER 7

Island Places

MAINE has been named the Pine Tree State, but Sarah Orne Jewett more aptly called the coastal part she knew, "The Country of the Pointed Firs." Along that coast, spruces rather than pines are the characteristic trees that have possessed the land since the ice age. In terms of human life, geological changes take place at an almost imperceptible pace, but in the time scale of geology the changes that have occurred in New England since the end of the last glacial period have been extremely rapid. Relieved of its burden of ice, the entire continent rose; but the glacial melt at the same time raised the ocean level, so that these two contrary trends more or less counteracted one another. Nevertheless, because of differential adjustments and tilting of the land, the shoreline was radically altered and is now what is called a drowned coast. Evidence of glaciation and rising land masses is easy to find. Erratic boulders, glacial scratches on recently exposed foundation rock, moraines, and old beaches high and dry on some hillsides all testify to these tremendous geological changes. As the ice retreated to the north, the bare land was revegetated, first by tundra grass and subsequently by the evergreens that have occupied the Maine coast since that time.

Penobscot is the largest bay on the coast; Great Spruce Head is in the middle of the bay and on the chart somewhat resembles a molar tooth—its crown pointing north, its roots south. Since circumnavigation was the easiest way for us to become familiar with the island, the names by which Great Spruce Head first became known were distributed around its shoreline. Before we visited any but the most obvious interior landmarks, we named every beach. Some names arose naturally from our first use of a place. Thus, Harbor Beach was the inevitable name for the sheltered south side of the Island where the dock was built, and off which our boats were moored; and Boathouse Beach for the evenly sloping, fine gravel extension of the harbor shore, above which a boathouse has stood from our first summer on Great Spruce Head.

As you progress counterclockwise around the Island, the next beach beyond the rocky headland where the Big House stands is Landing Beach, where the lumber for the house was brought ashore. Since the remaining features of the shore were named by my father and mother in their first year of Island exploration, there never was a time in my memory when they were unnamed. North Beach, at the foot of the Head, is followed by North Point, a bluff of bleached, flinty rock. On the northwest side of the Island, the Head drops precipitously into the bay. More than a century ago a fire destroyed the spruce forest that stood on this headland. From that forest the Island got its name. Now the head is covered with a mixed growth of stunted spruce and birch. Around this steep headland, winding through the forest and past mossy outcrops and wet cliffs draped with ferns, runs the path that circles the Island.

The steep bluff becomes more barren toward the west; dry lichens take the place of moss and ferns, and a vista opens onto a grass-covered point formed by a wide dyke of intrusive basalt that transects the Island. On the end of a ridge of broken rock where the dyke enters the sea, many generations of fish hawks have built a huge stick nest. This is Fish Hawk Point.

In the shelter of the south side of Fish Hawk Point, there is a small cove at the point of contact between the basalt dyke and the hard serpentine rocks of the Head. This protected cove terminates at a coarse gravel beach and a steep bank surmounted by a dense forest of big spruce trees. From a cleft in the bank, water trickles constantly into a small basin surrounded by a carpet of sundew. This is the only spring on the Island. When father and mother first visited this spring, they found nearby the bleached skull of a sheep and, in a romantic mood, named the place, The Beach Where the Indian Killed the Sheep. The name stuck, but has since been shortened to Indian Beach.

Continuing down the west side of the Island, you come to a series of beaches descriptively named Boulder Beach, Driftwood Beach, Skokie Beach, and the Three Island Beaches. Skokie, an Illinois Indian name for marsh, was the name given to the beach with a small cattail bog behind its gravel ridge. Three Island Beaches got their name from three tiny reefs off shore, two of which are connected to

[55

the beaches at low tide. This beach area is the western termination of lowland that extends across the middle of the Island from the harbor side.

Only a few feet above sea level, the lowland, once part of the Island's farmland, is now an alder swamp and a sphagnum bog. Year by year the alders have spread over more and more of the southern half of the Island, gradually converting it into swamp. The alder roots hold back water and prevent the rains from running off; the alder leaves block and absorb the sun, even on a hot day allowing only a golden-green light to filter down to the lower-story plants and the water-soaked land beneath them. Broadleaved skunk cabbages creak and rattle in the occasional breezes that penetrate this jungle, momentarily relieving the steamy, oppressive atmosphere. And here and there, on pools that dot the black muck of the swamp's floor, pithy-stemmed water arum floats, its startlingly white, lilylike spathes enclosing yellow spikes, each spike a multitude of true but undistinguished blossoms.

Around the Nubble, the hill on the Island's southern end, the trail passes only two small beaches. The first is below a graveyard where several early settlers of the Island are buried and is named Walton Beach after the predominant family name appearing in the graveyard. The second, even smaller beach, has no name. As around the Head, the path around the Nubble is built on a nearly perpendicular cliff for more than a hundred yards before it cuts inland and enters the western side of the South Meadow. The meadow slopes gently down to a beach facing Bear Island, after which the beach is named and to which it is connected by a tidal bar during the lowest spring tides. This beach was a campsite for Penobscot Indians before white men came. As witness to their long occupation, the Indians left above the high-tide line heaps of clamshells that are now sparsely covered by hawkweed and daisies.

From here the shore turns north again into a half-mile-long, narrow, tidal inlet that we have always called the Cove. At low tide the Cove is completely empty, exposing a mud bottom that is warmed by the sun when the tide is out during the day, and in turn warms the returning sea. On hot days, with an afternoon flood tide and southerly winds that blow the surface water into the Cove, the water at its end becomes very warm, often reaching the seventies, and is very pleasant for leisurely swimming. The height of the tides in Penobscot Bay varies between nine and twelve feet, so when the Cove is full, the water at its end is seven or eight feet deep. Since our first year on the Island, the Cove has been a swimming hole for children and adults alike; many of us learned to swim and dive there. When we were children, we swam there regularly, as did visitors from nearby Bear Island; our children learned to swim there and now their children are being taught to swim in those same Cove waters. Diving boards have been built and have disappeared, as have rafts and boats that were once anchored there as floats for the bathers; bridges, which suffered many casualties from the winter ice, were constructed across the narrowest place, below the swimming hole. Now only a single span without central pilings connects the two sides of the Cove. Essentially, though, time has wrought few physical changes. The trees and rocks remain the same; we dive from the same place on the bank as we did when we were children; and the summer sun, just as it used to do, still warms the flooding tide on a hot July afternoon.

Near the mouth of the Cove, on its western side, there is a semicircular sandy beach that at high tide encloses a small bay. We named the bay Sheep Cove after the remains of sheep that died there before we came. From the head of the Cove, the trail continues south along the Cove's eastern side to a small beach, behind which, in the woods, fishermen from other islands built a cabin to serve as a base for seining in the Cove and for scollopping in the waters around the Island. This is Fisherman's Beach. South of this beach the land rises more abruptly again. The path follows the contours of a wooded bluff until it emerges onto the Double Beaches, a gravel bar or tombolo littered with silver driftwood, mussel shells, and blackened strands of seaweed. The sharp-backed ridge slopes off on either side into smooth beaches that connect the main island to a small wooded knoll, called Pea Point by the natives. To complete the circuit of the Island, the trail follows the eastern shore of the wooded peninsula—the South Woods—from its termination at the Double Beaches back to Boathouse Beach and the harbor.

There are a few essential interior place names too. South Meadow implies a North Meadow and South Woods a North Woods. And there is a Sunset Rock, a shoulder of the Head. We often went there to watch the sun set behind the Camden Hills. But these features do not so clearly reveal the lines of time as does the shoreline, the face of the Island. Like the face of a man, it bears the lines and marks that the years have engraved on its rocky shores and beaches; and there much of its past is recorded—from ancient volcanic and metamorphic forces acting on its flinty core, to scouring by ice sheets out of the north and endless abrasion by the sea.

Dead tree on rocky shore, Butter Island

CHAPTER 8

Fog

THE ISLAND was a many-sided wonder, and its fog perhaps the most fascinating and characteristic of those wonders. It transformed and isolated the Island world, compressing it upon itself, leaving only near objects clear and unaltered. Everything else existed as dim, gray outlines, beyond which lay a thick and impenetrable obscurity that cut off the outside world. It often seemed, in fact, that that outside world had, for all sensuous purposes, ceased to exist. We moved in a muffling, wet grayness, through which, from somewhere, came the distant cawing of a crow, the echoed trumpeting of a gull, or the putting sound of a gasoline motor. But such sounds, during those gray hours, were not really an intrinsic part of our surroundings. Only sounds made by the fog itself belonged to us: the continual dripping from leaves and wet branches, the faint tricklings, and the less frequent, sudden, cascading shower started by some over-laden drop that finally broke loose from its moorings. Sometimes the fog lingered all day and the wind swept dense gray curtains of it through the trees. At other times, when there was no wind, the fog simply settled down like a great, white, woolly blanket. Often, the sun burned through by noon. As this slowly happened, the nearest neighboring islands loomed through the mist larger than they should have appeared, or they remained capped with lenticular clouds of fog while we were hot and humid in brilliant sunshine.

Before many summers had gone by, I had learned much about fog, the way it transmits sounds and the way it alters the appearance of familiar shores. I could take a small boat out in it and not get lost, although I might not land exactly where I had planned. I could set out for an island four miles away to collect the mail and find my way, if need be, without a compass. I even acquired a rough sense of time, so that I knew when to turn off the motor and listen for the sound of waves on a beach I could not see. It was usually possible to set out in the approximate direction I wanted by laying my course for the next landfall from the landmarks at hand. This island-jumping process almost always succeeded, although I did sometimes miss the mark and pass an island by without seeing a sign of it. I was never frightened, however, and was always sure of eventually making some land that I would be able to identify on the chart. To be out in the bay in a small boat—a white wall of fog narrowing your world to a fifty-yard circle of visibility—is, paradoxically, a broadening experience. Although the world you can see has shrunk, it is all yours— the boat and the little pond you are moving on is all you have—you are on your own completely and irrevocably; there is no calling for help; whatever happens is yours alone to deal with. The only companions you have are the occasional birds that fly overhead, and they are occasional indeed. When they come, you feel a bond with them, for they may be as much surprised by you as you by them. A low-flying gull or tern appears unexpectedly and looks around at you as he wings past. You feel he is a friend and greet him with a word or gesture. If he has come to investigate the strange sound he has heard, he probably will not answer; but if he cries out, you will, in your lonely world, feel reassured by his recognition and will know that you are at least in contact with some other life.

It is a tribute to the wisdom and forebearance of my parents that they allowed us to venture forth into weather they themselves would not have presumed to challenge.

We, my oldest brother and sister and I, spent a lot of time those first years exploring our little kingdom. Though the Island was only a mile long and barely half a mile wide, it was, in part, rugged enough and densely wooded enough to challenge our quest for adventure. There were many unique places, many rock-bound beaches to visit, and many routes to take from one place to another. We crossed and recrossed the Island, blazing trails to mark our way; and we climbed around the whole of the rocky perimeter, hiking through the woods and crossing patches of slippery seaweed at low tide. We set up secret hideaways, which did not long remain secret even from the adults to whom they were intended always to remain unknown. We reveled in our new-found freedom in a lush and abundant nature fragrant with wondrous, herby distillations. In our youthful thoughtlessness, we hacked and trampled in our paths the fragile things that today we would carefully step over or around. But such was nature's richness and fertility that the wounds were quickly healed. On the southern, sunny slope of the Head, then treeless, a mat of juniper and hay-scented fern grew. We loved to play in the thick, sloping beds of these ferns, rolling downhill through the fragrance of crushed fronds, the crackling dead stalks of previous years cushioning us from all but the biggest rocks and deepest indentations. My father looked askance at this game, which destroyed the new growth for the year, but he forebore to make much protest and never forbade us this pleasure. Our joy on the Island was unbounded and uninhibited, and time slipped by unmeasured. We lived in the unplanned present and so awoke with shock to the harsh reality of leaving at summer's end, and we wept.

One summer, because they decided we were not making the progress in school that we should have been making, our parents hired a tutor. A pleasant young college student, he lived with us the whole summer, and had the task of trying to fill in the gaps in our education. I was a particular target of this effort. Though I never resented the tutor, accepting his pedagogical demands submissively, that summer was the most painful in my memory.

Mother's sympathy for us—her concern for our joys and sorrows, aspirations and disappointments—was a grace founded on her own happy childhood. She seemed to understand perfectly our longings, our preoccupations, and our agonies. She did not rebuke us for failing to suppress them in times of childish stress, or when they interfered with the education and the development of self-control that are part of growing up. Instead she gave us support, encouragement, and kindness, and tried to assist us through the times of greatest trial. She helped me with my first-year high-school Latin and on my fifteenth birthday wrote a poem that epitomized, perhaps, more her own deep feelings than the anguishes of academic learning:

> *The Schoolroom walls enclose a little space*
> > *Where with bent head your docile thoughts all seem*
> *On Caesar fixed; the world without a dream,*
> *Forgotten for relentless mood and case,*
> *The Latin meanings patiently you trace,*
> > *Determined to forget some boyish scheme*
> *That waits the closing bell. Till sudden gleam*
> *Of sunlight on your book transforms the place.*
>
> *Then fly your thoughts to summer's treasure quest*
> > *Where white gulls flash against the arching blue,*
> > *And circling fish-hawks utter plaintive cries*
> *Above the loose sticks of their fledglings' nest.*
> *Star-lighted nights, awakenings in the dew,*
> *Summon you where a fog-girt island lies.*

That tutorial summer may have been the summer, too, when we had an epidemic of German measles that went undiagnosed until all of us had recovered. The circumstances surrounding the epidemic are curious. The island had become the focus of an infestation of brown-tail moth, a bud-worm that attacked the new spruce growth. It was believed, and it may be true, that the hairs of the moth's abdomen were very irritating to the skin and would raise an itchy rash. Since we were outdoors much of the time and came in contact with everything that grew, when we broke out with a rash on our arms and bodies, it was assumed that we suffered from brown-tail moth itch. We were never very sick, and if any of us developed a temperature, it went unnoticed. Not until a young medical student who had visited us for a week went back to Boston did the truth become apparent; he, too, had contracted the brown-tail moth rash. (Incidentally, that bud-worm infestation, which lasted for several years, finally disappeared without the aid of any kind of spraying, DDT being unknown then. Birds and other natural forces took care of it.)

Each generation of children belonging to a large, coherent, happy family has its own memorable period. Its members look back on it as a time when they pursued a particular activity with single-minded enthusiasm. In their later lives, the unusualness of this activity, their own ingenuity, or simply their wild enjoyment, makes this period a high point in their childhood. For me, and perhaps for my brothers, such a high point came one summer when we had visiting us several of our friends, both boys and girls. That summer we played the game of "Kick the Can" after supper, evening after evening, until it became too dark to see.

The farmer's boy joined in the game, and later his older brother. When he first came, he joined in without any formal introduction, as is always the way with children. For the game's sake, however, if for no other reason, we had to be able to call him something, and his younger brother said, "Call him Bert." In our preoccupation with the excitement of our play we misunderstood, and he became known as Columbert, a name that stuck to him all summer, even after we learned that his real one was just Bert. Columbert, being a rather strange name, was discussed by the family at meal times; but since the children in Maine seemed to us often to have rather unusual names, it was never seriously questioned. A controversy, however, did spring up over its pronunciation. We children maintained that the accent was on the first syllable, whereas father, maintaining that the name was derived from Columbus, insisted that the second syllable should be accented—a very silly way, we thought, to pronounce it. Bert

Orchard in the fall, Great Spruce Head Island

Hay fern, Great Spruce Head Island

himself didn't enlighten us, accepting any rendering of Columbert without protest. When eventually the truth came out, the question of pronunciation became moot; father never said another word about it, nor did the rest of us. But we continued to call him Columbert.

Many years later, when my younger sons and the children of my brothers spent successive summers on the Island, they started a form of play that developed from simple beginnings into a most elaborate and imaginative game. To us, their parents, it became a beautiful spectacle.

It all started with swimming off the beach near our wharf, where there happened to be a plentiful supply of drift logs and timbers. At first, each boy secured for himself a large log on which to lie while he paddled around half-submerged. From this beginning, the logs were stabilized with outriggers, making it possible to sit on them without tipping over. Then, under the stimulus of rivalry, larger and larger logs were acquired and combined into rafts on which the boys could even stand up. Superstructures were added, and paddles made for propelling these primitive craft. Inspired by the novelty of what they were doing, they built for their ships elaborate harbors of stones, and landing docks on flimsy piles. Nails, always a scarce item on an island, became invaluable and were exchanged at premium rates. Rusty ones were salvaged from old crates and timbers and carefully straightened, and many odd pieces of scrap iron were used as fittings on the rafts. The game became highly organized: groups of rafts were formed into rival navies and sophisticated rules were developed to govern combat. Raids on rival bases and fierce water fights took place. There was never any great danger of mishap because the rafts could not sink or be upset. If the captain-crew was pushed overboard in battle, he could easily scramble back over the mere inch of freeboard.

Invention has traditionally been credited to necessity, but no less has it been mothered by the search for labor-saving improvements and by ambition. Under the impetus of these less commonly recognized incentives, sails were introduced into the fleets during the second summer, revolutionizing their locomotive power. The rafts sprouted masts with stays and halyards, and all the old torn bed sheets on the Island were requisitioned for sail and banner. On days when a gentle breeze ruffled the blue surface of the bay, the fleets would sally forth, bright flags waving and ingeniously makeshift sails straining against their sheets. They would cruise sedately around the harbor, making good progress before the wind, but returning under paddle power.

As the minds of the young seafarers turned to more peaceful pursuits, naval engagements diminished in frequency. Their eyes sought the distant horizons; the irresistible lure of adventure and exploration possessed them. The first expedition planned was a cruise down the coast of the South Woods to the Double Beaches, a long half mile. In preparation for this voyage, all the vessels were overhauled, refitted, and stocked with provisions for a day. Then, when the augeries were propitious, they set sail—not quite at dawn. The expedition returned late the same day, all participants elated, all objectives gained. Encouraged by the success of this enterprise, they mounted a second expedition—to turn the cape of the Double Beaches, enter the Cove, and explore its farthest confines. This undertaking called for more thorough planning. Not only did the winds have to be taken into account, but the tides had to be considered as well, for the Cove could only be navigated when full. As the explorers themselves might have predicted, the winds and tides caused no difficulty; the second expedition was brought off with dispatch.

These coastwise explorations, however, much like the Portuguese voyages down the west coast of Africa in the fifteenth century, were not sufficiently challenging to the explorers. The imagination of a Columbus was needed to sustain and carry them forward from enterprise to enterprise, and they all were Columbuses. The next compelling task was to cross the "Atlantic" between Great Spruce Head Island and the Barred Islands and press on to the uninhabited land of Butter Island. The stretch of water between our Island and the chain of islets to the southeast is a watery waste of treacherous currents and fickle winds, but our intrepid sailors crossed it with a dash and spirit never before known in the annals of Great Spruce Head Island. They attained their first goal, the rocky, forbidding coast of the nearest of the Barred Islands, and continued on undaunted—on through the dangerous, reef-infested narrows that divide the Barred Islands into two groups; on, finally, to the distant, beckoning, white beach on Butter Island, where, a mile from their homeland, they landed and planted their flag.

Following Columbus, there had to be a Magellan. The last expedition of the summer was the circumnavigation of Great Spruce Head Island. The most careful planning and all the skill and accumulated know-how of rafting went into that improbable voyage. For four miles, with favorable and adverse winds, high seas, and strong currents running against them, the voyagers struggled on from dawn to dusk. As always, they came home triumphant. After that miracle of navigation, there was no daunting them. They were planning to take their strange craft to Camden, an awe-inspiring twelve miles away on the mainland, when the summer, fortunately, ended.

CHAPTER 9

Matinicus Rock

NOT FAR from Seal Island, and also exposed to the full force of winter storms, is a group of other islands of which Matinicus is the largest. Matinicus Rock, the site of a lighthouse, and the outermost, loneliest rampart, rises above the Atlantic from the continental shelf five miles seaward from Matinicus Island. On this pinnacle of split and shattered granite, above the reach of the surf, puffins, black guillemots, and arctic terns come yearly to raise their young. Sharing the islet with them are Leach's petrels, pelagic birds that nest in burrows they dig in the sparse, peaty soil, and that return to their young from ocean foraging only at night. They come to land only to breed and rear their young, otherwise living entirely upon and above the surface of the oceans. Petrels incubate their eggs longer than any other birds, with the possible exception of some of the penguins. Yet once they have fattened their young on the energy-rich, oily plankton that they scoop from the surface of the ocean, they desert them, even though they are unready to fly. The young continue their development to adulthood on stored reserves of fat, obtaining no more food until they are able to forage for themselves.

After the death of my parents I had the opportunity to visit Matinicus Rock. With the relaxation of military security following World War II, I became the guest of a very agreeable and hospitable Coast Guard crew and spent a week on Matinicus Rock photographing birds. I slept in the lighthouse dormitory and took my meals at the board with the men. One staple of diet that I appreciated more than they was lobster. Day and night there was always a dish pan of freshly boiled lobster kept warm on the back of the stove. To this delicacy and to coffee, the rule was to help yourself at any time. The lobsters were provided by fishermen from Matinicus Island, who would stop at the lighthouse slip and leave some whenever the sea was not running too high. The crew, which had been eating lobster in this quantity for months, was understandably sick of it and much preferred red meat; but I, even though I had enjoyed lobsters frequently during the summer, had not yet reached their stage of surfeit, and I stuffed myself on them.

The coast guardsmen were all young and very eager to help me with whatever I wanted to do. I suppose they found my presence and activities a relief from the boredom of routine. Any request I made was immediately granted. My second story dormitory window gave a view each morning of the sun rising across the island. It was a magnificent sight to see the orange disk burning through the fog and spreading a soft light over rocks and outbuilding. I wanted to photograph it, but I was frustrated by a dirty storm window outside and a painted-shut sash inside. At breakfast one morning I mentioned the situation, and before I knew what was happening the men were all out with a ladder removing the storm window. They broke it in their haste, but the mishap did not dampen their enthusiasm; with their flattering good nature they said that the photograph would be well worth it. The inside sash put up more of a fight, but even it succumbed quickly when the men applied a chisel to it. The next morning I got my picture. All this was done under the supervision of the petty officer in charge of the station. His name was Waters. So of course his nickname was "Salty." Another time, when I was trying to photograph the lighthouse itself at dusk, I realized that to get the effect I wanted I would need a double exposure. The first exposure had to be made just before sunset, and the second after dark when the light was on. But the rules for good lighthouse tending require that at all times during the day the lamp and its lenses be protected from the sun by curtains. If this precaution is neglected, the rays of the sun will focus through the lenses onto the lamp filaments, and, in a reversal of the usual direction of the light, could damage them. I discussed the problem with one of the men, who volunteered to withdraw the curtains before I made the first exposure and replace them immediately afterward. He insisted that no harm would be done to the lamp because the sun's rays late in the day would be too weak to do any damage; and besides, he said, he would remove the lamp first anyway. So, late in the afternoon I set my camera on a tripod and

[63]

Arctic Tern, Matinicus Rock

got ready for the picture. The young coast guardsman was in the lighthouse tower, and when I signaled to him he pulled up the curtains and I immediately made the exposure. Several hours later, after dark, I returned to make the second exposure for the light in the tower, and the composite picture was completed.

I went to Matinicus Rock expressly to photograph puffins, but because I came late in the season most of the young birds were already out on the water and I was unable to find any occupied nests. The terns, however, still had downy young running about and the young petrels were many weeks from fledging.

Matinicus weather is usually foggy in summer. Nearly every night during my visit the fog would roll in and the lighthouse diaphone would start up its fifteen-second rhythm. I had no flash equipment for photographing birds at night, but I sat up every evening on the rocks near a group of petrel burrows to watch the birds come and go. In the intervals between the whumping of the horn—while the circling beam of light came rushing toward me out of a wall of fog, flashed past, and rushed away on the other side—I would listen for the petrels returning from the sea. They would come like huge moths, only dimly visible in the fog-reflected light, and plunge, twittering softly, into their burrows. So ghostlike were they that I was never quite sure I had really seen them; but I felt their presence and heard faint calls, and sometimes was brushed by air from their wings.

In the daytime I photographed the terns. Since I wanted pictures of them in flight, I set up my blind in the center of their nesting territory. In tern colonies there is always much noisy conflict over territory and an incessant, high-pitched *kee kee keearr* of birds coming in from the sea with fish. Terns hover before alighting, looking for their own place in the colony and for their young. My plan was to photograph them at this moment. It proved more difficult than I thought it would be because the young birds did not stay in one place and because there was scarcely time to focus accurately on a hovering bird. As a solution, I conceived a stratagem to force them to hover always at the same distance from the camera. I found a weathered whiskey crate washed up among the rocks and placed it in front of the blind; in it I put a young tern. Its parents soon found it and from then on alighted on the edge of the box or hovered above it before dropping herring to the young bird within.

For two days I photographed arctic terns. The fog was thick over Matinicus Rock and all my photographs at first were made against this white background. But in the afternoon of the second day the sun burned through for a short while. During this interval a tern paused above the whiskey crate, treading the air with its wings. With the sun pouring through his feathers, he glowed like a white flame. And I had the picture I wanted.

My interest in birds, which has continued undiminished, began with a childhood preoccupation stimulated by the many new varieties abundant on the coast of Maine. At first, only the larger birds drew my attention. They were the most conspicuous and could easily be identified without field glasses. Not until many years later did I begin to appreciate the wealth of species of song birds that inhabited our Island and the neighboring islands during the summer. To me, as to most children, they were merely a background of sounds and small, elusive, flitting bodies among the trees. A few songs sung at dusk, however, did stand out and became magic symbols of Great Spruce Head Island. The sweet, high-pitched, deliberate whistle of the white-throated sparrow, and the ascending, liquid warble of the olive-backed thrush were evening songs that, even as a boy, I quickly learned to recognize. Thereafter, whenever I heard these songs, I felt a melancholy nostalgia. They evoked visions of mossy woods, meadows, and lichened rocky slopes, reinforced with fleeting odors of evergreen forest and sweet fern.

I found, accidentally, a few birds' nests beside the trails, or stumbled on them in raspberry thickets in the course of gathering berries. Not until I was grown to manhood, though, did I purposefully set out to know the birds that lived on the Island, to learn their songs, and to find their nests. Before that time, there was enough to observe about the obvious birds to hold the attention of a boy. At low tide, gulls and crows were always foraging for crabs and shellfish in the seaweed along the shore. The gull, snowy white and spotless, is visible for half a mile and can be heard trumpeting to his fellows as he pecks for food. From time to time he flies aloft with a shellfish, drops it on the rocky beach to smash it open, and follows it down to eat it before it is retrieved by another gull. The crow struts jerkily among the seaweed-covered rocks, alert for anything edible, muttering to the other members of his band, and occasionally punctuating his remarks with sharp, staccato caws.

Around the perimeter of the Island, in the woods above the shore, the fallen needles of spruce and balsam form a brown, springy bed of forest duff that fills the hollows between the loose stones and exposed roots of the larger trees. Maianthemum—wild lily of the valley—and star-flower are the first flowers to bloom there in the spring. There also, in the grass on exposed promontories, where juniper lies flat over the jagged rocks and orange lichen

Boathouse, Matinicus Island

Lighthouse, Matinicus Rock

grows in scaly patches, you find the crows' scattered refuse. From the aggressive gulls, the crows retreat with their catch to the comparative safety of the higher wooded ground, there to feast undisturbed. All along the path that follows the Island's shore are strewn the fragments of marine animals: bleaching clam shells, powdery from long weathering; fading blue mussels; greenish pincushion sea urchins, some with their spines still on; carapaces of crabs dragged from their hiding places beneath the rock weed; and chips and pieces of legs, claws, and spines. In places, accumulations of these remains suggest a communal banquet, where crows had gathered, if not to share the repast that each had retrieved from the sea, then at least to share the society of other crows.

Undisturbed by the quarrels and flurries of the crows and gulls, great blue herons from a rookery on another island wade the shallow waters of the Cove in slow motion, stalking the small fish that stay in the undrained, warm pools at low tide. But the most magnificent of all the large birds is the osprey, or fish hawk, the hawk that dives for his food. That first summer in Maine seven pairs of ospreys nested on the Island, one pair on the top of a dead spruce in the interior, and the other six on rocky points and islets around the shore. One of these nests, the one on Fish Hawk Point, had been occupied so long that a structure of sticks four feet high and more than three feet across had been built by annual additions through the years. Changes in the past fifty years have left only one osprey nest on the Island. A shrinking fish population in Penobscot Bay has partly accounted for this loss, but the widespread use of DDT-type insecticides, which diminish the osprey's fertility, has also been an important factor.

All the other nests, one by one, year by year, have been abandoned, and even in the big nest on Fish Hawk Point the eggs laid this year and last failed to hatch. Inevitably, and soon, the year will come when no hawk returns in the spring to lay her eggs and rear her young.

Fish hawks were so characteristic of Penobscot Bay during my childhood that they made in my mind the same deep impression as did those first experiences on the Island. They could always be seen circling over shallow water at low tide, searching for fish. From my bedroom, which overlooked the bay, I often watched them. At dawn sometimes their piercing cries would get me out of bed; I would stand at the window hypnotized, watching a bird hover as it spotted a fish, flap laboriously to hold its position, and then slide into a dive that spiraled down to the final plunge. With wings partly folded and talons extended in front of its head, it knifed into the water with a minimum splash, disappearing from sight. Ospreys are reckless birds that on rare occasions become entangled with fish too large for them and so are drowned. Knowing this, I always waited anxiously during this critical and seemingly interminable moment, wondering if the bird would reappear. He always did, though not invariably with his quarry. Out he would come, beating the water with his wings and trailing a ribbon of drops as he rose, and, if he had struck accurately, holding in his talons a very lively fish. After rising some distance, he would shake himself doglike to remove the water from his feathers and then, sailing off, announce his success by a series of piercing whistles that were echoed by his mate as he approached his nest.

I spent many days in a blind with my friend, Fairbank, photographing fish hawks at their nests, watching them return with their catch, and witnessing the welcome they received. With much excited screaming, the mate on the nest would fly off to meet the returning bird, and together they would alight to share the food. First, however, they would tear off morsels for their young. Often we crouched in our blind fearful to make the slightest move, lest the fierce-eyed hawks so near at hand detect our presence and take alarm. They would stare in our direction with unblinking yellow eyes, moving their heads from side to side to gain a better perspective until we were sure their keen sight had penetrated the very fabric of the canvas.

Through the first quarter of this century, dense beds of eel grass grew from Penobscot Bay's muddy-bottomed, shallow coves, where a foot or more of water remained at low tide. The streaming green ribbons of this plant could foul a propeller more effectively than a lobster pot line or a trailing rope. At high tide, waving stems of eel grass rose in thick forests almost to the surface; at low tide, the grass stems floated over the shallows in interlacing strands, through which rowing was difficult and driving a motorboat impossible. Eel-grass beds provided a nursery for many kinds of fish. Safe from many of their enemies, but not safe from them all, mackerel and herring developed there from fry to sizeable fish. To the eel-grass coves, terns would come to hunt food for themselves and their young. All day long they would fly back and forth from these fishing grounds to their colonies on the treeless islets scattered through the bay. They would congregate over the shallows where the fishing was good, hovering, diving, and incessantly screaming at one another about their success, or lack of it. Maneuvering with grace and speed like a swallow of the sea, a tern can hover, suddenly plunge toward the water, change his mind in the last split second if his quarry escapes him, and pull out of the dive a hair's-breadth from the surface. Or a contest may develop, the tern that caught a fish being chased by one that missed, the chaser trying to frighten the chased into dropping his catch. Sometimes there is a twisting, weaving race, the pursuer following with incredible agility every elusive turn and trick of the pursued, as though the two birds were controlled by a single brain.

The terns were as dependent on the eel grass that harbored the fish they preyed on as some owls are dependent on meadow grass that shelters the mice they hunt. They carried away in their black-tipped beaks thousands of wriggling rainbow-hewed minnows with no noticeable depletion of the supply. In the twenties, a plague struck the eel grass and it began to die all along the New England coast, leaving coves that had been choked with its tangled filaments clear and free, a welcome sight to boatmen. The disappearance of the eel grass, however, altered the entire ecology of the area to the disadvantage of both the fishermen and the terns. Without the grass, there were no shallow-water nurseries, and fish became less and less plentiful. With starvation facing and overtaking the terns, they abandoned their old haunts. Their colonies shrank in size until finally no nesting birds were left and the only terns seen in Penobscot Bay were non-breeding individuals returning for a meager subsistence. How far-reaching the effect of the ecological disaster was I do not know, but it seems to have brought about many changes that could not have been foretold. With the death of the eel grass and the disappearance of the herring and mackerel, flounders also disappeared. When we were children, it took us only an hour or so to catch enough flounders from the harbor to provide a meal for the entire family. During the past twenty-five years, however, hardly a one has been taken. The fishing habits of the ospreys changed too. From a dependence largely on flounders they were forced to switch to other fish, soon making pollack their commonest food.

At the same time, affected also by these profound changes, a bird seldom seen before became abundant in the bay. It was the double-crested cormorant, or shag, as it is usually called. It settled in the gull colonies, pre-empting part of the gulls' territory; it occupied some of the former tern islands; and it took up residence on islands not previously colonized by birds. Cormorants are the long-necked, black birds often seen skimming low above the wave tops in twos and threes and in single file, or perched in solitary watchfulness on buoys and spindles, wings spread wide to dry. They build bulky stick nests in dense rookeries on the ground or in trees. Wherever they congregate to breed, all vegetation is destroyed by the corrosive richness of their excretions. The rocks, the spongy soil, even the sticks of their nests are encrusted with a gray-white layer of bird lime, and from all comes the pungent odor of decomposing fish. Fertilized by the nitrogen-rich effluence, nettles and mustard plants grow to enormous size on the fringes of the nesting areas, although they cannot survive in them. And the trees in which the birds build their nests are soon converted into gaunt, leafless skeletons, suffocated by the deposits that coat them from top to bottom.

Out of pale blue eggs, mottled with a chalky white deposit, black, shiny-skinned, and naked reptilian young hatch. At this stage of their development, the approach of man or bird stimulates an automatic response. Like a gaping, sessile marine animal, or some grotesque, carnivorous, primeval flower, each membranous throat opens wide and waves feebly in expectation of food. In their parents, a feeding response is instinctively aroused by this behavior. In ignorant and prejudiced humans, however, it usually has quite the opposite effect, merely increasing the revulsion already felt at the hideous aspect these young birds present before their first down appears.

When seen close at hand, cormorants present an appearance much different from the one they present at a distance. No longer are they entirely black. The skin of their throats and lower mandibles is orange-yellow, their feathers are marked in a fine filigree pattern of iridescent greens and browns, and they stare around out of glass-green eyes. Moreover, though they are reputed to be voiceless, when at their nests they respond to their mates with a hollow, gutteral croak.

The activity that goes on at a cormorant's nest is especially fascinating. The young are fed by a regurgitation process in which they insert their heads into the gullet of the parent bird, which forces fish from its crop, by spasms, directly into their mouths. One young bird at a time is fed in this way on partly digested food until the reserve supply is exhausted. The parent then usually leaves the nest to resume its underwater fishing. When the young are small, the adults normally take turns at the nest, the foraging bird often being greeted with much hollow croaking when it returns. Occasionally, the incoming bird brings a stick to its mate—a persistence of its behavior during the nest-building ritual. Birds wet from fishing often perch near their nests before feeding their young, their wings stretched out to dry in the wind in the same spread-eagle pose they so commonly assume on spars and spindles around the bay. Hours spent in a cormorant rookery in the concealment of a blind could never be tedious; something new, different, and expressive of the individual traits of the birds that surround you is constantly taking place.

Waterfront, Matinicus Island

Fishermen, by and large, do not like shags, and on occasion raid their colonies, destroying their eggs and young. I once saw such a raid through binoculars from a mile away on the north end of the Island. Horrified, and helpless even to protest the wanton destruction, I watched two men land on a cormorant island and systematically go from nest to nest smashing eggs and clubbing young birds to death. I asked a fisherman friend why they did it. He replied, "Do you like them awful things?"

To speak of the ugliness and corruption in a bird rookery is not an impartial observation: it is a biased judgment. It carries the implication of emotional involvement and very possibly moral condemnation. From one outlook, nature is neither ugly nor beautiful, offensive nor pleasant, good nor bad: nature simply is. But this Olympian view is never consistently possible for mere mortals. Even for the most scientifically unemotional individual such heights of detachment are far from attainable. Though it is true that in nature without man no moral precepts exist, they are introduced by him, who is part of nature, because it is his nature to do it. As a result, he becomes trapped in the cage of his own inner convictions, which require that he feel and judge.

Yet, by striving to be free of these self-imposed bonds and escape his limitations, man is able to attain, in some few compartments of his self, an objectivity that is a measure of his comprehension. Paradoxically, with this comprehension comes an emotional quality to man's participation in the whole complex of nature—a kind of happy acceptance of the world as it is—that in the end becomes an overwhelming desire to see nature remain unaltered, except by its mindless forces.

The early morning breeze was still blowing, and the warm, sunshiny air was of some ethereal northern sort, with a cool freshness as if it came over new-fallen snow. The world was filled with a fragrance of fir-balsam and the faintest flavor of seaweed from the ledges, bare and brown at low tide in the little harbor. It was so still and so early that the village was but half awake. I could hear no voices but those of the birds, small and great—the constant song sparrows, the clink of a yellow-hammer over in the woods, and the far conversation of some deliberate crows.

—SARAH ORNE JEWETT

CHAPTER 10

Becoming a Photographer

I BEGAN photography, I suppose, as so many photographers have, with a Brownie box camera. It was given to me at about the time we started going to Maine, not because I wanted a camera, but because some adult could think of nothing else to give me for Christmas or a birthday. My father, however, might have given it to me because of his own interest in photography, an interest that began when he was a young man with the invention of the Eastman roll-film Kodaks. He took one of those cameras with him on several camping trips to the Canadian Rockies and filled an album after each trip with the photographs he made. We children would look through the albums with great absorption, taking special interest in the pictures of our parents and their friends in their camping clothes. There was one album, not of the Canadian Rockies, that fascinated me in particular. It contained a whole series of pictures of the construction of our Winnetka house, from the first breaking of the ground to the final planting of trees. I was born in this house a year after its completion, so, in a sense, its construction also marked the beginning of my life.

As I recall, I first used the Brownie with pleasure in Maine. Before that, I may have taken some pictures of birds' nests in the shrubbery beside our driveway in Winnetka, but the nests never showed up very well. My first pictures around the Island were imitations of pictures father took, always unsatisfactory landscapes or shots of coasting schooners we passed on our first cruises on the *Hippocampus*. It wasn't long, however, until I began to photograph the nests and young birds we saw on the bird islands we visited. Young gulls and gulls' eggs were big enough to show up at six feet in a Brownie picture. Captain Green would take the exposed rolls to the drugstore in the town of Deer Isle when he took the laundry over and would bring back the processed pictures the next week. Each week I experienced a good deal of excitement in anticipation of the results, and was very disappointed when the pictures were light struck or blurred, or did not show what I expected.

My first photographic success came during the summer we were tutored. Several of us children, accompanied by the tutor, visited a colony of great blue herons on Bradbury Island at a time when the young herons were well grown. As we struggled through the fallen trees overgrown with raspberry bushes in the middle of the colony, a young bird about to fledge took alarm, flew from its nest above our heads, and crashed in a nearby raspberry thicket. It stood there half-buried in the bushes, its long neck stretched out and its crest feathers raised, glaring at us in fright. I took a picture of it, with the help of the tutor, and it turned out to be one of those accidents of photography in which every variable works in favor of the photographer. The picture, which showed in sharp detail the fierce eye and raised feathers of the angry bird, so impressed and pleased my father that he had an enlargement made of it.

After that, I tried photographing the fish hawks on North Point and the Double Beaches from a small tent-like blind I had devised, and mother had sewn up for me out of green cloth. The blind worked all right, but the results were very disappointing. Only those pictures in which a hawk was standing quietly on its nest were sharp; all those of birds in flight or alighting were completely blurred. The tenth-second shutter speed of the Brownie was entirely inadequate for this kind of work.

On the next Christmas, I was given the newest model Kodak with a top speed rating of 1/300th of a second. Equipped with this instrument, I returned to the ospreys the following summer. This time my best friend, Fairbank, went to the Island with me. Together we squeezed into the tiny blind, patiently waiting for hours to photograph the hawks. We took many pictures, and many were excitingly good. With one I won a twenty-five dollar Eastman Kodak Company nature photography prize. My winning photograph was reproduced in posters and distributed to drugstores and photo supply shops all along the coast. But to my disgust the Eastman advertising department, in spite of my protests, called it a picture of an eagle.

The next step up in equipment, after several more years,

72]

Double-crested Cormorants, Colt's Head Island

was the acquisition of a Graflex, which I bought myself with savings from my allowance. Fairbank also had one. Together we visited the gull islands, spending days in our cramped quarters with only a meager lunch and a thermos of water to sustain us from sunrise to sunset. The gull pictures we took then did not survive, but I remember them for their dullness. They mostly showed gulls standing on rocks in the distance, like milk bottles left on the kitchen porch. When it came to terns, however, we did better. They seemed to be more tame than the gulls, and when they alighted on their nests paused momentarily with their wings extended in graceful photogenic poses.

By this time I was so deeply involved in photography that I wanted to do all the processing myself. During the winter, at home in Winnetka or away at school, neither time nor facilities for this kind of activity were available; but on the Island I had the time, if I could find a place for a darkroom. The small basement room where the hot-water heater was located, under the east end of the house, was the only feasible place I could find. Water was available, and with a minimum of labor the room could be made light-proof. Father gave me permission to install a small sink, and in a few weeks I had set up a laboratory. I had had no previous experience with film processing and over-ambitiously purchased a variety of developers, thinking that I could work out my own formula. Not surprisingly, it didn't turn out to be as easy as I had expected and many rolls of film were underdeveloped. Finally I settled on a standard prepared developer. I never did much printing in this darkroom because the profligate use of water that photography requires was not permitted, but for two years I did develop roll film in a tray by inspection. As my interest in bird photography waned during my college and medical school days, the darkroom was allowed to fall into disrepair. It was not until years later, when I had a house of my own on the Island, that I built another small darkroom, which I still use for loading film.

After I graduated from medical school in 1929 and, under the inspiration of Dr. Hans Zinsser, still had the ambition to become a bacteriologist, I became a close friend of one of my classmates who did photography as an avocation. Influenced by him, I bought a Leica and began again to do photography in my spare time. I was not so interested in birds then as in a more abstract approach to subjects illustrated in the photographic annuals of those years. I photographed leaf patterns, details of bridges, splashing water, and close-ups of many everyday objects. As time went on, I accumulated a modest collection of prints, and one day was invited to show them at a friend's house near Boston, where a visiting photographer from the West also would show his pictures. Although I was at first flattered by the invitation, the occasion, in the end, became for me a very embarrassing one. More important than that, however, it was an experience that had a profound influence on my subsequent work. The western photographer was Ansel Adams, and the photographs he exhibited one by one on an easel took my breath away by their perfection and strength. Never had I seen any photographs like them. I wanted nothing so much at that moment as to forget my poor photographs and keep them out of sight, for I knew they would be the anticlimax they proved to be when I finally unwrapped them. Ansel Adams was very kind. Sensing my embarrassment, he looked at them all, made several helpful comments, and suggested that I use a larger camera.

I did not immediately take his advice. Instead, I tried to revise my technique of printmaking to obtain the Adams quality, and continued to photograph a great deal in the summers. One fall several years later, my brother Fairfield, who was studying painting in New York, introduced me to Alfred Stieglitz, whom I visited later at his gallery, An American Place. He looked at my latest photographs and told me they were all woolly, but that their fault was not a matter of sharpness. I didn't understand what he meant unless it was a matter of sharpness and decided then to get a larger camera. Periodically, after that, I went to see him with the best work I had done since my last visit. He was always encouraging, but also noncommittal, cautioning me that photography was very difficult and required much hard work. At last, while looking through the box of photographs I had brought to him early in 1939, Stieglitz stopped suddenly and said, "You have arrived. I want to show these." It was completely unexpected; I was dumbfounded. But I was thrilled, too, for all at once I knew I was indeed a photographer. Later, after the exhibit, Stieglitz wrote this letter about the pictures on January 21:

My dear Eliot Porter:
I have your letter. I have been wanting to write to you but have been swamped with people & "things." And I am far from being physically equal to the demands I make upon myself—I think I know how you feel about me. *Men* really don't have to thank each other.—Still I must thank you for having given me the opportunity to live with your spirit in the form of those photographs that for three weeks were on our walls.—And "our" includes yours.—Some of your photographs are the first I have ever seen which made me feel "there is my own spirit"—quite an unbe-

lievable experience for one like myself— . . . Once more my deepest thanks to you & Mrs. Porter. Also the same from O'Keeffe.
                Your old
                    Alfred Stieglitz

And a week later he wrote:

My dear Porter: Thanks for your grand letter.— It is most welcome.—Your photographs told me all you are. Your letter is but a corroboration of those photographs. Crowninshield was in & I showed them to him. He had asked me what it was in the young generation that was so cold—so unfeeling. I showed him your prints as my reply. "He has your kind of feeling," he said, as he saw the first.—He looked at all & said: very, very beautiful . . . I understand fully how you feel about your work & how you must follow your inner voice— . . .

My warmest greetings to you and your lady—
                Your old
                    Stieglitz

Obviously, this exhibit in January of 1939 marked a changing point in my life. I made up my mind to give up research in medical science, a field in which I had not been very successful, and give myself fully to photography.

Having made this decision, there were no compelling reasons for living in Cambridge or Boston, so my wife and I decided to strike out into new territory and chose Santa Fe, New Mexico, as the place to spend the next winter. In the meantime, I had again become interested in birds. With a portfolio of black and white photographs, I went to Houghton Mifflin to see if they would be interested in publishing a book of bird photographs. In spite of my naiveté, I was courteously received by the editor-in-chief, who advised me that to be a success a photographic bird book should be in color. I accepted the challenge, though it seemed like a terrific undertaking with uncountable years of work. Since Kodachrome had recently been introduced on the market, however, it was not an impossible task. From Eastman Kodak Company I got some helpful suggestions about flash photography with color film, and after the winter in Santa Fe I applied for a Guggenheim Fellowship to photograph birds in color. It was granted in the spring of 1941, and with it began the many years, not yet ended, that find me each spring devoting all my time to bird photography, from Arizona to Maine, and from Minnesota to Florida.

Double-crested Cormorants, Colt's Head Island

Osprey and young, Great Spruce Head Island

CHAPTER 11

Nests

WHEREVER I was there was always deep in the back of my mind a network of impressions of our Maine island—all its essential shapes, colors, and smells. They persisted through the summer the family went to Alaska and the Canadian Rockies and through the summer I went hoboing in the West on freight trains and worked in a lumber camp. In recent years I have not been back to the Island very often but the buried images have not lost any of their sharpness.

Before going to the Southwest with children of my own, I built a house on the Island and became more seriously devoted to photography. Each time I visited Alfred Stieglitz I took evidence of my expanding photographic interest —from birds to the Island itself, and finally to the whole bay, with its towns, houses, people, and boats. Eventually, a closer focusing on the details of the woods and all living things—on flowers, mosses, ferns, and lichens—brought me back to my original photographic subject, birds. The song birds became my special preoccupation. Among them, the large family of warblers drew my closest attention and has held it ever since, from one end of the country to the other.

Finding bird nests is a skill for which all the guide books, all the geographical check lists and life histories, and all the learned volumes on ornithology are of little help. Despite the assembled knowledge on territorial behavior and nesting activity about any species, to find a nest still requires patient and painstaking observation that most ornithologists are unwilling to practice. Only for relatively few birds have the details of breeding and nesting behavior been recorded, and then only for a few individual pairs in one or two localities. But behavior varies greatly from individual to individual and from place to place. Instead of being concerned with the hard-to-define lore of nature, ornithologists today are more interested in taxonomic and evolutionary relationships, for which the gun is a more useful tool than the camera. It is easier to record electronically the difference between territorial and nesting songs than to describe complex breeding behavior. That behavior, for example, may vary in pattern from pair to pair according to the period in the nesting cycle; and it may be more or less conditioned by the presence of an observer. Although many behavior studies have been made, they contain mostly observations amenable to tabulation and measurement. They answer questions of rates and quantity, but give very little information on quality. You are told how much, how many, and how often, but are given no experienced opinion on the why and the wherefore, questions that are strictly not for science. These questions are ignored because emotion is something that the scientist has done his utmost to eliminate from his mind. By abstracting himself, he abstracts his subject. It is not permissible to impute love and hate, or joy and sorrow, or even anxiety and contentment to a bird. An ornithologist does not acknowledge that a bird has emotions. A bird is only a bundle of reflexes and instincts to him. Nevertheless, because birds behave as though they did have emotions, because they appear at times nervous and anxious, distressed and unhappy, or at other times joyful and exuberant; and because these qualities are manifested by them while they are raising their young, they have a meaning in terms of which bird behavior is interpretable.

The nest finder must go out into the fields and woods with his wits sharpened to a razor's edge, with all his senses tuned to their highest pitch, and with his mind free from the distractions and preoccupations that burden the society he has temporarily left behind. His consciousness must be focused on the world outside himself, in which he must move without self-awareness. If he succeeds in attaining this rapport with nature, all creatures, as Thoreau said, will rush to make their report to him. He will learn who his companions are, where they are, and what they are about. All their activities will be as shouted declarations, and no secrets will be kept from him.

I wandered through the forests and bogs and alder thickets from dawn to dark, day after day, and summer after summer, listening and searching, tense as a taut wire for the slightest vibration and flick of movement. Unaware of time, I moved through the day without plan or design, following the trails and random leads laid out by nature. At sunrise I waded through dew-laden redtop grass that soaked my sneakers and legs, and crept through bushy thickets from which drops showered down on my face, neck, and back. Often I was drenched before the warming sun had dried the leaves. I went out in fog and rain all day and returned late in the afternoon, without a dry spot on my body, but neither cold nor uncomfortable. I found many birds' nests and knew the locations of many more. I felt that I had established a speaking acquaintance with an alder flycatcher whom I had seen place in the fork of a blackberry vine the first yellow stalk of grass for her nest, and who "peeted" at me from furtive concealment when I visited her later from time to time. And for the little redstart whose mate sang from the very top of a slender white birch, I felt a tender solicitude. From the cunningly fashioned, gray fiber nest in the alder crotch, she warmed her pearly eggs wreathed in violet and brown, and returned my gaze, fearful and unblinking.

Some birds nest on the ground, where I have come across them unexpectedly. On occasion, from almost under my feet, a tiny, brown, mouselike creature would scuttle away swiftly through the vegetation on the forest floor. Reaching down among the leaves, because I knew it was no mouse, I would uncover a nest of eggs lined with the finest grasses or with the shiny, reddish fruiting stalks of mosses woven into it. Often it would be sunk in the ground beneath some overhanging ferns, where no eye could find it from more than a foot or two away. On other occasions, the bird would jump away, awkwardly fluttering over the ground to distract my attention, its wings drooping in feigned injury, and all the while mewing in distress. These breath-stopping moments, when my heart raced with an intense and startled excitement, would freeze me to immobility for fear that a false move would inadvertently destroy the nest I had so nearly stepped on.

Like the bird population on Great Spruce Head, certain lichens thrive on the Island both in the trees and on the ground, their growth aided by the salty, foggy atmosphere of the Maine coast. Just above the highest tides a brilliant orange variety splashes its color over the rocks, making streaks and circles in greatest profusion where the shore is most exposed to spray-laden winds. Amid the upland rocky outcrops and thinned-out stunted spruces, gray, branching reindeer moss fills all the crevices and hollows. In dry weather, these miniature forests crackle under foot; but when wet, they become a spongy elastic cushion. The most profuse and obvious of all the lichens is the usnea, or misnamed beard moss, of the northern forests. Every spruce tree supports some of it, and like the spruce, it, too, seems to thrive must luxuriantly on exposed headlands, festooning and smothering the trees with its trailing streamers, branched and waving threads, and gray-green knotty clumps. Not a parasite like mistletoe, which sucks its nutriment from its host, usnea is an epiphyte that uses the trees for support.

Usnea is used as a nesting material by many birds, but only one has adapted its habits to the lichen's manner of growth. This bird weaves the hanging strands into a pendant pouch, to which it adds a few spears of grass for the lining, but no other material. It is the little parula warbler, whose name has been given to the Parulidae, a new-world family of warblers that has one hundred and twenty members. The soft, blue and gray plumage of the parula warbler, dabbed as though haphazardly with bright canary and mustard yellow, blends in most agreeably with the pale gray-greens of the lichen. To find the nest of a parula, one must spend the day among the festooned trees, sitting quietly and listening attentively for its song. It may be necessary to move about from place to place because the males are not very persistent singers and their song does not carry well. It is a sibilant song, an insect buzz that is blurred by the sounds of the wind in the trees and is carried away and lost entirely if it originates a short distance to leeward. Once the tiny singer is located, however, it is almost certain that somewhere within a few hundred feet, in a denser than usual mass of usnea, there is a nest. To find this needle in a haystack, one needs only patience; sooner or later the birds themselves will point it out. But one must watch them constantly and not let them escape from sight. You may spend a day or you may spend many days, but in the end I will guarantee that if you have kept your wits clear of the fog of drowsiness and your eyesight sharpened to a pinpoint of concentration, the warblers will show you where they live. It will be easier to locate the parulas' nest when they have young, for then they will be busy carrying small caterpillars and other food to their offspring. From some point of vantage, the destination of one of these journeys will be revealed.

The eider duck is another bird that builds its nests of unusual material, but to find them you have to explore the neighboring grassy islets. One half mile out from Great Spruce Head Island a chain of islands guards its eastern shore, providing a sheltered harbor against all but the severest northeast storms. These islands are called the Barred Islands because, except for a winding channel that separates the northern two islands from the southern members of the group, they are all connected at low tide by muddy gravel bars. Only two of the Barred Islands are wooded, the others being grass-covered islets with a few scattered trees.

Olive-back thrush, Great Spruce Head Island

The northernmost of the islets, because of its rocky, pointed profile, has always been unofficially called Peak Island. On these small, barren islands, safe from most predators, eider ducks come to nest in the early spring. In order to find them and the early-nesting, solitary great black-backed gulls, I went to the Island one May before spring had really got under way. The air was still chilly, even in the sun, and the birches and alders were bare, giving the deciduous woods a gray transparent appearance as though seen through glass. Only skunk cabbage bloomed in the bogs, its curiously mottled, reddish, introverted spathes pushing out of the unfrozen black muck around the alder roots. A few migratory birds had arrived, among them the myrtle warblers and one or two of the sparrows, but the great migration hordes had not yet come and few songs resounded to gladden my winter weariness.

One day after breakfast, soon after I had arrived from Boston, I was sitting on the Farmhouse steps in the crisp morning air looking down the beach to where the rocks became overtopped by the dense spruce forest. The interlocking branches of the most forward trees seemed to hold back the forest from spilling into the sea. Yet here and there the continuity had been broken by the undermining action of waves and storm, and a tree, losing its grip, had toppled over onto the rocks below. It was not a friendly, gentle quality that one felt in these pointed trees, but a painful adaptation to an austere and hostile land. Since the tide was out, I was acutely aware of the sweet, decaying, weedy odors of the beach, odors that mixed with the resinous scents of evergreens into a familiar, experience-evoking combination. Odors elicit total recall, unlike the other sensations, which need confirmation to establish the authenticity of a remembrance. We hear a bird sing and look around to find the source of song; or we see a man chopping at a great distance and listen for the sound of the axe to verify our sight and give the action reality. With odors it is not the same; when re-experienced they bring back the whole of the past, recreating in the brain an image of the place and action at the time the odors made their first impression. And so as I sat there in the morning sun, these elusive odors recalled from past summers many visions, which flashed before my mind like pictures on a screen.

No softening signs of spring were yet perceptible here. I shifted my sight from the cold gloom of the woods, repelled by their forbiddingness, and looked away across the glittering water to Peak Island. A boat had come into view through the Barred Island passage and was headed over toward me. I had heard the sharp, quick beat of its motor for quite a while as it approached from the other side of the islands, but now I could see it, a dark speck bobbing over the wind-scuffed waves. It came down the broad path of the sun, the usual values reversed by the white glare reflected from a multitude of short, shifting waves. The breaking crests were dark against the intense light. The white boat itself appeared black; the spray from its bow, as it slapped the tops of the waves, fanned out on either side into dusky translucent wings, studded and bordered with drops that caught and projected to me the rays of the sun. In spite of the scene's sharpness, all detail of the boat was obscured by the contrasting brightness that surrounded it.

As it moved out of the glare, becoming more distinct, I saw that it was Earl Brown's boat. Earl Brown was a fisherman from Eagle Island who often came over at low tide to dig clams or to visit his sister, Lottie Howard, the caretaker's wife. He was an old friend, who looked upon my activities with an amused, tolerant condescension spiced with good-natured kidding. He himself knew a lot about the wildlife of the bay, although for fear of being kidded about what he thought to be a rather childish interest, he would not admit it. I went down to the shore to meet him and reached the beach just as he stepped out of his punt. We exchanged our usual chiding, sardonic greetings and I asked him what he knew about the eider ducks. He didn't think they were nesting yet; the drakes were still hanging around. When nesting begins, the male birds depart for the rocky outer islands and the open sea, leaving incubation and care of the young entirely to the females. The drakes don't return until the following spring. Besides, Earl said, the spring had been colder than usual; everyone was complaining about it. Mornings would start off nice like this one, with the promise of a fine, warming day, but by afternoon a cold wind would blow up from the south, taking all the warmth out of the sun. The prevailing winds along the coast are southerly. They blow in off the Bay of Maine, bringing fog in the summer and warmth from the Atlantic in winter. But often in the spring, when the land is warming up faster than the ocean, they blow chill and cheerless—right off an ice cake, as the fishermen say.

Earl picked up his hoe and clam barge from the bottom of the punt and started off down the beach. Neither of us spoke a parting word. It wasn't necessary.

I stood on the beach, undecided. It was quite rough, but the distance straight across to the Barred Islands was only half a mile. If I rowed over now, the wind would not be against me, as it probably would be later in the day when it had swung around to the south. Perhaps I might find an early duck's nest after all, contrary to Earl's predictions.

Earl Brown, Eagle Island

It was worth investigating.

Once in the rowboat and away from the shore, I changed my mind. Instead of rowing over to the nearest of the islands, I veered to the northeast into the eye of the wind and headed back the way Earl had come, towards Peak Island. It would be harder work and would take longer, but I was in no hurry. The blades of my oars, every now and again on the forward stroke, sliced into the top of an oncoming wave, cutting off clusters of drops that the wind caught, blew high, and pelted down on me. My skin became all knobby with gooseflesh, the first defense against cold; uncontrolled shivering comes next. But with the bright warm sun beginning to temper the crispness of the morning, the chilly spray on my neck, cheeks, and bare arms was exhilarating rather than unpleasant.

As I approached Peak Island, I had to cross a narrow deep-water channel that leads between some ledges into Barred Island harbor. This small haven, safe in all weather for even fair-sized sailing boats, lies in the grasp of the two wooded members of the group, Big Barred Island and Harbor Island. Two of the ledges in the channel that are exposed at low tide are used as basking rocks by harbor seals. This morning more than a dozen of all sizes crowded onto the larger of these rocks. As they dry in the sun, the coats of the older animals change from a dark gray to a light sandy color, and their bodies seem to stiffen, their heads and tails raised like curled flakes of cracked mud. When I came into sight beyond the end of Harbor Island and entered the channel, the seals wriggled and flipped off into the water, singly and by twos and threes. Those down near the water's edge slid in silently with hardly a splash, but those higher up on the rock humped themselves down vigorously and tumbled in with a great commotion. After a few minutes, their round, sleek, earless heads soundlessly began to appear. At a safe distance, and on all sides of me, the seals rose to breathe and to look me over, and then silently sank from sight again.

Seals have a reputation in the bay for more than usual intelligence. Earl Brown insists that they can count to seven, an ability that he claims to have proved. Mackerel and herring fishermen who have fish weirs—offshore traps built of stakes, brushwood, and nets—are constantly at war with the seals. In pursuit of fish, the seals often get into the weirs and tear the nets. The fishermen shoot them whenever they find them around their weirs, and when the destruction the seals cause is especially great, try to eliminate the seal colonies from the neighborhood. The most effective way, one would think, would be to attack them on their basking ledges, but that is not as simple as it seems. If a man lands on a seal rock, the seals will leave and, even though the man conceals himself, will not return until he has left; nor will they return if he is landed by a companion who then rows off. According to Earl, as many as seven men can land and leave one of their number behind with a gun, and the seals will not be fooled. Only when seven men depart will the seals finally return, to be shot by an eighth.

Once past the seal ledges, I turned toward Peak Island. Since the south side of the island is a mud flat at low tide, considerable skill is needed to make a dry landing there. Nevertheless, because this side was in the lee, I now thought it a better place to land than the steep rocky shore exposed to wind and waves. I rowed in hard in order to drive through the mud as far as possible and, just before sticking, jumped to the stern to raise the bow and so thrust the boat forward a few more feet. I finally stuck fast about twenty feet from the beach in three inches of water. By shoving with an oar, rocking and hitching the boat forward, I succeeded in working it ahead to within jumping distance of dry ground. Then, taking the end of the painter in my hand, I leaped from the bow, landing well up from the edge of the water, but not on as firm ground as I had hoped. Mud spurted out on all sides and my feet sank into it over the tops of my sneakers. Since they were now muddy as well as wet, staying out of the water was pointless, so I waded back to the boat and pulled it up onto the beach. The water was very cold.

I found two eider duck nests. One, containing four very large, greenish eggs, was on the beach in an accumulation of driftwood. The other, containing two eggs, was in the grass above the beach. The soft gray down in which the eggs are nestled is plucked by the female from her breast. Before she leaves her nest, if she is not too suddenly alarmed, she pulls some down over her eggs, providing them with protection against both discovery and cold. One might expect that this flimsy cover would blow away with the first puff of wind, but in fact it takes more than a gale to strip it from the eggs. Every downy feather has barbs equipped with rows of minute hooks. When interlocked, these hooks hold the whole mass together, and hold on as well to sticks, grass, and other objects around the nest with an amazing tenacity. Such is the solicitude of the female eider for her offspring that if her first nest is robbed she will provide this downy insulation for a second and even a third nest, at considerable sacrifice, it would seem, to her own warmth and comfort.

On my way back to the boat, I stopped to watch and listen to some savannah sparrows. They make their homes on these bare, wind-swept islands, building their well-concealed nests deep in the tangled grass. They arrive early

[83

Savanna Sparrow's nest, Peak Island

in May, apparently enjoying the boisterous, chilly spring days, and remain until late fall, when the grass has faded once again to winter straw. On a windy day, they flutter downwind like dead leaves from one clump of grass to another, playing what seems to be a carefree game of tag. On reaching the shore, they fly back to the other side of the island in one bold dash to start the performance all over again. During their game, they alight on dead stalks or tufts of weeds and sing weak, wispy songs that are swept away by the tumultuous air. Stroking the grass, whirling the birds along and dispersing their songs, the wind echoes a plaintive whisper, faintly heard above the wild sounds of unendurable loneliness.

May is also the time of year when the woodcock return. How and from where they come I do not know, for I have never seen them in migration flight, or resting on the shore, or in the open fields like the shore birds. In fact, I have never seen them anywhere except in their chosen habitat. But suddenly, one day, there they are on the Island, and there is no mistake about it. Undoubtedly, they arrived during the night, but by what giant leaps from bushy pasture to bushy pasture they winged their way up the New England coast is a mystery to me. At twilight, amid budding steeplebush and sprouting fiddleheads of fern, they search for food, probing the soft, fertile pasture soil with their long, sensitive bills. From a hidden place, a male and female bird begin their courtship. The male begins with a harsh, nasal "pamp" repeated at moderate intervals, and then, as though no longer able to contain his ardor, takes off in flight. For an hour at a time in the gathering dusk, I have stood with my arms on the top rail of a pasture fence, listening to and watching the woodcock's nuptial display. Even in the dark you know when the flight begins, for it is announced by a whirring of wings.

Around in a big circle the male flies, spiraling up into the faintly lighted sky, a black fluttering speck. His arc narrows with the crescendo of his beating wings until, straining at a pinnacle in the evening air from which he seems unable to fly higher, he pauses, hovering there in silence. Then, like the emergence of a butterfly from a chrysalis, a new creature is born. From the summit of his soundless striving, the woodcock dives to earth, leaving the heavens behind, and pouring out in soft, rich warblings all his pent-up joy. Down he comes in long steep arcs, a falling leaf with an angel's voice. He comes to earth beside his mate, no doubt at the place from which he had taken flight a few moments before, and begins again his unmelodious "pamping."

CHAPTER 12

Voices in Spring

IN THE MINDS of most people, spring is associated with flowers and birds. Robins and some of the hardier birds appear early, when snow is still on the ground but brown earth and last year's withered grass is beginning to show in patches. The gurgling, tinkling sounds of water from melting snow and ice can be heard as the clucking of a robin and his first song uplifts the spirit. But these sounds are merely harbingers of a spring that still is far away. Winter will lash back again out of the north, bringing snow and freezing weather. And the birds will sit with feathers fluffed up to endure the cold, disconsolate and waiting for a change, wondering, perhaps, what had happened to the spring and why they had come so soon. But spring will advance nonetheless, silently and unnoticed. These rearguard actions of winter will be repulsed in the end; the higher sun will assert its dominance through the longer days, and the winds will dry the fallow land wherein a million shoots from the seeds of last year's growth are slowly stirring.

The first flower that breaks into bloom in the snow-covered northern woods is arbutus, its pink and fragrant flowers clustered about with the still-green last-summer's leaves. Then the shad blooms before the leaves have broken their buds, looming ghostlike through the gray forest's trunks. At the same time, red maple buds deliver their petalless flowers to fall and strew the black forest puddles with spidery dots of red. But there are few maples on the Island, so white birches take their place and are the first to be brushed with green. The hillsides and bogs, where white birch trunks stand above the gray-stemmed alder thickets, become feathery with pale new leaves before the catkins appear. This phenomenon of the rising sap can be duplicated on a thawing winter day, I am told by Rupert Howard, if one sets a match to the shredded papery bark of a white birch. The flame will leap up the trunk, briefly warming the whole tree before burning out; and the next day, if the thaw continues, all the buds will open and put forth new leaves. The death of the tree, however, is assured, for its cycle has been upset and its spring has come too soon. Sometimes cycles are upset by natural causes: I have seen a yucca in the west bloom in September and a horse chestnut bloom in October in New England.

An alteration of normal cycles can be induced by other kinds of interference. Once I raised several generations of Polyphemus moths from cocoons, but during the spring and early summer of the second generation I had to be away. To keep the moths from emerging in my absence, I left the cocoons in an icebox until my return in July. Two weeks later the moths hatched normally, mated, and the females laid eggs. It was so late in the season, however, that the caterpillars had insufficient time to develop at their normal pace. When September was well advanced, they still were not fully grown, and the oak leaves on which they fed were beginning to turn brown. I was forced to search far and wide for still-green leaves. Some constituent necessary for continued growth must have been lacking in those old leaves, because the caterpillars stopped eating while still undersized and one by one spun miniature cocoons. The next spring miniature moths emerged, stunted by an inadequate diet and by my disturbance of their normal growing cycle.

When the month of May is well advanced, a New Englander may look for the arrival of the first great wave of migrating birds. It is an event of considerable consequence and involves in its most spectacular aspect that colorful family of new-world birds, the wood warblers. As the leaves unfurl, the vanguard of the later-migrating hordes begins to arrive, a few early warblers and many sparrows of different species. The casual observer of the spring realizes that birds are singing again. He will say, "I heard a song sparrow today"; or, "What was that new song I heard this morning for the first time?" But to those for whom birds are a hobby or a profession these events will long have been noted. These people are out early with their binoculars to identify every new arrival by sight and by song. They have also been waiting for a certain morning, that morning on which the trees are suddenly alive with birds, all busily foraging for insects that have appeared with the first leaves. Through the short moonlit night the new arrivals have flown. They are hungry after their exer-

Harbor and shore, Great Spruce Head Island

Bunchberry flowers and lichened rocks, Butter Island

tions and must renew their bodies for the next lap of the journey north. Were it not for the food they find during their daytime pauses they could not continue their flight, and would perish from starvation. The next year their numbers would be less, and after that, if the shortage of food continued, there would be silence in the spring.

In incredible thousands, birds occupy every tree, fluttering from branch to branch in a feverish search for insects. Warblers by far outnumber all other kinds. The first waves are the males, identifiable by their gay plumage and their songs. All day long on the Island, and day after day for several weeks, I have watched them, sought them out, and determined their kind. They come in all colors: orange, yellow, brown, greenish hues, blue, and occasionally red. Of the many combinations and patterns, blue and yellow predominate in myrtles, magnolias, Canadas, and parulas. With few exceptions though, they all are marked with some yellow, which varies from the total yellow of summer warbler to the crown, rump, and small yellow flank-spots of the myrtle. The songs, too, seem infinitely varied. Some, high-pitched and buzzy, are near the limits of hearing, like those of the blackpoll and bay-breasted; others are rich and melodious, like the yellow warbler's or the throaty song of the Canada. And in between these extremes—a multitude of other songs.

At dawn the chorus begins. I awake early, and from my bed listen to the announcement of spring and count the number of songs I can hear. Some, right outside the window, are loud and insistent. A black-throated green warbler is trying to get me out of bed with his strident, simple notes, and farther away another is singing a different version of the same theme. Faintly, in the distance, I hear a magnolia, and can also make out the sibilant buzz of a parula and the weaker, warbly song of the myrtle. Then nearer again I hear several redstarts. But behind and through all these separate songs a constant chirping, peeping, and rustling forms a background of indistinguishable sounds that attest to the thousands of night arrivals. Since the waves of birds began—for several mornings now—I have been hearing new songs at the start of each day. I identify some old friends who have returned for the summer; and I recognize, too, the songs of Blackburnians and Cape Mays, birds who pause at the Island only for a rest and are gone with the night in a day or two. Warblers are not all I hear, however, for mixed with their songs are those of red-eyed vireos, whitethroats, purple finches, wood pewees, crossbills, and the cheerful, ebullient ruby-crowned kinglet. I am unable to lie in bed, for I must see as well as hear the throngs that have taken possession of the Island during the night. Once out, I find it hard to concentrate on any particular bird. Everywhere, in all the trees, especially among the tender new leaves of the birches, is a seething mass of active, brilliantly-feathered little bodies. My eye is caught by a flash of orange and black, and my subconscious automatically registers "redstart," but my mind cautions, "Are you sure it is not a Blackburnian?" As I hastily try to bring the creature into the field of my binoculars I catch a glimpse of a black necklace about the yellow throat of another bird. I switch to him to make sure I saw a magnolia and not a Canada, and now the orange one is gone. In desperation, I lower my glasses and stare at the tree, not knowing where to look next and not really caring because I know they are all there; I have heard their songs. Sooner or later it is certain each kind will pop into view, and unless I hear a strange song my eyes would only confirm what I already know. Nevertheless, for a long time I wander, hungry for breakfast, but unwilling to return to the house, unwilling to disengage myself from this wondrous phenomenon of life that recurs each year.

From the jungles of South America, over thousands of miles, these tiny birds wing their northward way, undaunted by the hazards of ocean wastes, or the wastes of civilization. Instinct impels them to reproduce their kind in their ancestral lands. To what is this annual two-way mass movement a response? Perhaps it is an adaption to the advent of the ice age scores of thousands of years ago. But think of the casualties there must have been in those past eras; how few must have survived the year-long winters of snow. And from those that escaped have evolved the present families and species. Every year since the retreat of the ice these growing families have returned to their old homes, and by so doing have given to their kind the scope to multiply freely, away from the overcrowded tropics. Perhaps somewhere buried in the depth of their brains there has survived through these ages an ancient memory, an intense, vital spark, a pattern of cells that initiates and controls their return. Here they all were, returning by the billions, like living waves beating against the retreating winter, now only a symbol of the ice that covered this land not so long ago. They occupied every available island, gathered in unusual concentrations along the coast, and spread over the whole breadth of New England. Every wood, hill, and farm was this day ringing with the songs of these uncountable numbers of birds. This is indeed the mystery and miracle of spring.

CHAPTER 13

Reunion

I WAS eleven years old during my first summer on Great Spruce Head Island in 1913. In 1963, after a lapse of eight years, I went back to the Island with two of my sons, their wives, and four grandchildren to take part in a fiftieth anniversary reunion. On July 20 of that year, an eclipse of the sun swept across Maine and out to sea late in the afternoon. The path of totality crossed the northern part of Penobscot Bay, touching the Island. Deciding that this event would be an appropriate one for the reunion celebration, my sister and brothers and I sent out the invitations. Friends and relatives from near and far who had visited and knew the Island during the past half century were asked to gather with us for an Island open-house, and to watch the eclipse. They came from all over the bay that day, and from more distant places; or paused on their cruises to eat and drink with us. The harbor was crowded with fishermen's boats and sailing yachts, more than had ever gathered there before. It was a warming and congenial affair, and the celestial phenomenon that was obscured by clouds in many other parts of the state was clearly revealed to us. Not with the pure, unobstructed clarity hoped for by astronomers, since a high film of cloud intermittently blurred the sun, but in a beautiful and dramatic display. From the top of the Island we saw the foreboding shadow of the moon rushing towards us out of the west, and, just before totality, a last flash of light through a lunar canyon. During the instant of maximum darkness, the surrounding horizon glowed with an eerie, orange fire as the earth seemed to hover on the brink of extinction. This was a moment when savage, atavistic fear was not far below the surface.

But many strong feelings had awakened beneath the surface of my consciousness before I had arrived at the Island. As I drove along the coast of Maine that June, through all the pretty little villages and across the many tidal inlets that I had not seen for many years, I was seized by an increasing excitement. The day was perfect—as bright, warm, and blue as the unforgettable day of my first Island trip fifty years before. I was, in a sense, going home; but more than that I was re-experiencing a vast, unsounded, and unrecollected accumulation of buried memories. My excitement derived in large measure from unrecognized past experiences that never fully came into view, but that somewhere in my subconscious initiated a chain reaction of emotions. Had they come to the surface to be recognized and placed in their proper order, those feelings would have had a rational foundation and might have been less intense.

I stopped in Camden, our old familiar base of supplies, stocked up with groceries, and visited the wharves, my nostalgia rising to even higher peaks of intensity. Inexplicably, I felt anxious as well as excited, as though I feared that the Island out there in the bay might no longer exist, and perhaps never existed outside my imagination. From a few places near Camden, however, the highway rose above the foreground of trees and afforded a view of Penobscot Bay. At these points, the blue bay lay stretching away to distant land and to a hazy merger of water, sky, and fog. In the middle-distance darker blue, lenticular islands floated on the streaked, ground-glass surface like ships of a great fleet at anchor. And there, confirming my recollections, its top showing above the nearer-lying ones, was the dim outline of the Island, only a dozen miles away by water, but one hundred still by road. That final lap of my returning journey was interminable. At last, however, I arrived at the little settlement of Sunset on the opposite side of the bay from Camden, only six miles from Great Spruce Head. I left my car there and continued on in the mail boat that runs from Sunset to the Island during the three summer months.

At last, unbelievably, I was on the Island. It had not changed: everything was the same. The trees towered as they always had, their dark pyramids of spreading branches spaced carefully, from those that touched the rocky ground to the spire at the top. The grass path up to my house was still not trampled down into a worn, brown carpet as it

Sensitive ferns and raindrops, Great Spruce Head Island

would be by many treading feet through the summer. The odors of spruce, fern, and salt sea were heavy in the air. Suddenly, all tension was gone out of me, and I felt content. All I wanted to do was lie relaxed in the grass and look up at the tree tops and the sky; but a son and his wife had preceded me by two weeks and were there to welcome me, so I did no such thing. They were brown and happy, and I bubbled over about being back at last. We talked about nothing in particular, and I asked them innumerable questions about their doings, about which, of course, they could give me no account. What one does on an island in the spring cannot be related. Words cannot describe the soaking up process that goes on, the flashing impressions that go to make up the day and night. Indeed, why did I so crave repeated confirmation of what I already knew? Why, after sharing an inspiring experience, are we compelled to talk about it in banal and meaningless terms?

For the next few days I poked around into the old familiar corners, savoring the woods and the meadows full of sweet grass, hunting up venerable knotted trees, and tracking down the half-hidden vines of honeysuckle-sweet twinflower. By following the twinflower's perfume, which pervades the forest far around its beds, I found the flower itself, cascading over half-buried boulders or interwoven in moss on old stumps, and I put my face to the blossoms to breathe their fragrance deeply. But I also found, contrary to my first impression, that nothing remains the same for long, that nature is in constant flux, and change is the only permanent condition. Winter storms had leveled colonnaded stands of branchless forest trees, exposing to the sun a litter of fallen trunks and raspberry thickets. The abandoned pasture was invaded by an impenetrable growth of vigorous young spruces. Our blueberry and strawberry beds were disappearing under the advancing forest, which had already taken over the hillside slopes of bay, brake, and hay-scented fern. The birds, too, were different: the ospreys were almost all gone; veerys had taken the place of hermit thrushes; crossbills, which years ago were never seen, were now extremely common; and starlings, like an invasion of ill-mannered picnickers, were all over the Island, their raucous bickering going on from daybreak to dark. The starlings had pre-empted all the hollow trees and were driving the flickers from their own nesting holes. Cowbirds had at last discovered the Island and were parasitizing many of the smaller birds. Even the warbler populations had changed; new species had moved in and old familiar ones were no longer heard.

Yet these were normal manifestations of the dynamism of nature, which is never static for long and cannot be contained within a framework suited to our conservative prejudices. If we hack away in an attempt to trim the world to fit a constant mold, nature responds by redirecting her vigor into a new activity. She does not defend her positions, as the advocates of the need to conquer her imply she does; on the contrary, she bends and accommodates and adjusts, reacting in many subtle ways. If in our smug ignorance we cut into her too deeply with our machines and chemicals, she retreats before the attack to a new position, as though saying, 'If this is the way you want it, you may have it so.' But it may turn out to be a way we do not at all anticipate. Nothing is more self-flattering than the power men wield over nature. They are frequently rewarded by spectacular success, as in agricultural productivity. On the other hand, the misapplication of limited power based on half-knowledge leads all too often to unwanted results, the consequences, for example, of many of the pest-control programs. In other areas of exploitation and control of natural resources, disaster to both man and wildlife has been a more common outcome, and we have often been deprived of what we cherished most. Nature is never confined: she has no limits, no ultimate stand, no last resort. For nature, there is no Thermopylae or Alamo. When man, abetted by climatic changes, has in the past laid waste a land once teeming with life, nature accommodated by introducing lizards that swim in the sand, rats that need no water, and trees without leaves.

On the Island—a few hundred acres of Maine land—interference and manipulations by man have been kept to a minimum for half a century. Untrammeled nature responds there to her own forces with little human interference. There one may watch nature freely manifest herself in the chain of succession from one living form to another, from season to season, and from decade to decade. Birth, germination, growth, and death follow an inevitable sequence. A tree becomes a fungus, the fungus becomes soil, and soil a new plant. The leaf is food for an insect, which in turn is food for a bird. Over a longer period of time, some forms of life disappear and new forms are introduced. Why these changes take place is a puzzle for which there may never be a solution. Perhaps, as observers, the greatest knowledge we should ever expect to acquire is the what and how of these changes.

During the reunion summer of 1963, I re-experienced much that I had previously learned about the Island, and I experienced many sensations heightened and made perceivable by my years of absence. I got up before sunrise, when an early morning mist, full to overflowing with light, lay like thin wool over the islands. I saw the sun rise red out of the eastern horizon, and saw it scatter a strip of glittering golden tinsel down the wrinkled bay as it rose. I

Water arum and ferns, Great Spruce Head Island

watched the sky and water slowly change from purple to luminous orange, while gulls sat on offshore rocks waiting for the ebb of the tide. And I saw the sharp silhouette of a boat—a lobsterman on his early rounds—cut smoothly through the path of the sun.

I watched, too, the nights deepen over the scattered islands in our corner of the bay. What a different world they made. On a moonless night the sky ceases to exist; its place is taken by the enormous firmament of stars, bright in an immense, black infinity of space. When the wind is down and phosphorescence runs high, the glow of myriad organisms softens the cold fixed reflections of the stars, sunk deep in the inky water. Night is a simplification: the world is drawn down to its bare essentials and the distracting details disappear, leaving only the bold outlines of objects. But the black emptiness of night is peopled by the uninhibited imagination, and mystery crowds in wherever the imagination is given scope. The most familiar places, only dimly perceived in the dark, change their dimensions and content so radically that one begins to expect completely unrecognizable things to ooze out of the blackness.

There are other changes as well, changes in the dimensions of relationships that seemed settled and familiar. For if one is privileged to live through the cycle of two generations, he has an opportunity to gain a perspective on his life, first through an emotional attachment to his children, and later through a more detached involvement with his grandchildren. Free of the everyday problems and decision-making that beset parents in bringing up children, the grandparent enjoys a less routine relationship with the young people. Since a grandfather comes only intermittently into the lives of his grandchildren, and on a less authoritative level than the parent, he is able to build a new dimension by indulging both himself and them to their mutual enjoyment. The children bestow on him a confidence, received in different form from his own children many years before, that opens new vistas to an understanding not merely of childhood aspirations, but of his own childhood. Because it educes a latent tribal feeling of fulfillment, it can be a comforting relationship.

In the presence of my grandchildren, I was treated by my own children with the deference due a patriarch, a new sensation for me and probably for them too. Because of the grandchildren, they felt the spread between our generations more than I did. Most of the time I did not feel that I was a member of an older generation than theirs, especially when without protest they allowed me to wash the dishes as my part of the household chores. Only when they were solicitous of my comfort or deferred to my wishes did I feel the gap. But it was not an unpleasant sensation, and I made the most of it, basking in the warm atmosphere of close family ties and affection.

I realized, too, that along with all the other changes that had taken place on the Island went changes in the point of view of the inhabitants. The young people did not enjoy the Island as my generation had. Their interests were directed by a more complex technology that brought the Island closer to urban civilization. With that closeness, that loss of remoteness, the Island's wildness was ebbing away.

Farmhouse, Great Spruce Head Island

Island Color

MORE LAND THAN SEA

> There is, one knows not what sweet mystery about
> this sea, whose gently awful stirrings seem
> to speak of some hidden soul beneath.
> —Herman Melville

Sunrise from the dock, Great Spruce Head Island

A tree's significant when it's alone,
Standing against the sky's wide open face;
A sail, spark-white upon the space of sea,
Can pin a whole horizon into place.

—Dante Gabriel Rossetti

Barred Island from Double Beaches

Tidal Bar, Barred Islands

Lighthouse, Matinicus Rock

But the first salt wind from the east, the first sight of the lighthouse set boldly on its outer rock, the flash of a gull, the waiting procession of seaward-bound firs on an island, made me feel solid and definite again, instead of a poor, incoherent being. Life was resumed, and anxious living blew away as if it had not been. I could not breathe deep enough or long enough. It was a return to happiness.

—Sarah Orne Jewett

Its voice is always in the ear, sometimes subdued and wooing, sometimes as murmurous as the slow breathing of a sleeping beast, sometimes as wild and clamorous as a battle cry. All other sounds—the calling of birds, the wind over the heath, the speech of men—are flute notes against the deep orchestration of the sea.

Here the people seem to possess the secret of tranquillity and to live lives of more than surface contentment. That is rare today. Perhaps it is only by going up the old back roads leading to the lost little hamlets of the mountains or the seagirt islands and peninsulas of the world that you can still find it. Perhaps even in such places it has not long to last. . . .

—Louise Dickinson Rich

Mustard and rock, Colt's Head Island

Blue lobster buoys, Maticinus Island

Yellow lobster buoys, Stonington

The children also go about collecting empty bottles—pop bottles, beer bottles, grape-juice bottles, any bottles of pint or quart capacity. Wooden stoppers are whittled to plug them tight, and they are attached to the lines that run from buoys to traps at a point about eight feet from the buoy. It used to puzzle me to see, at low tide, each bright buoy accompanied by a floating

Green bottles, Matinicus Island

bottle; but now I know the reason why. At high-tide the bottles are submerged as the lines run straight to the floor of the sea; but as the tide ebbs they rise toward the surface, picking up with them any slack that might otherwise snag on the rocky bottom and hinder hauling. It's a simple, ingenious device.
—LOUISE DICKINSON RICH

But above all it is the fantastic colouring of the beaches that as an image overpowers the minutiae. Above the tideline the grey rocks are splashed gorse-yellow with closegrowing lichen, and with others of blue-green and salmon pink. Beneath them are the vivid orange-browns and siennas of wrack-weeds, the violet of mussel-beds, dead-white sand, and water through which one sees down to the bottom, as through pale green bottle-glass, to where starfish and big spiny sea urchins of pink and purple rest upon the broad leaves of the sea-tangle.
—Gavin Maxwell

Barnacles, Great Spruce Head Island

Down on the shore we have savored the smell of low tide — that marvelous evocation combined of many separate odors, of the world of seaweeds and fishes and creatures of bizarre shape and habit, of tides rising and falling on their appointed schedule, of exposed mud flats and salt rime drying on the rocks.

—RACHEL CARSON

Algae in splash pool, Isle au Haut

There is a perpetual mystery and excitement in living on the seashore, which is in part a return to childhood and in part because for all of us the sea's edge remains the edge of the unknown; the child sees the bright shells, the vivid weeds and red sea-anemones of the rock pools with wonder and with the child's eye for minutiae; the adult who retains wonder brings to his gaze some partial knowledge which can but increase it, and he brings, too, the eye of association and of symbolism, so that at the edge of the ocean he stands at the brink of his own unconscious.

—Gavin Maxwell

THE BAY'S EDGE

My life is like a stroll upon the beach,
    As near the ocean's edge as I can go;
My tardy steps its waves sometimes o'erreach,
    Sometimes I stay to let them overflow.
My sole employment 'tis, and scrupulous care,
    To place my gains beyond the reach of tides;
Each smoother pebble, and each shell more rare,
    Which ocean kindly to my hand confides.
I have but few companions on the shore,
    They scorn the strand who sail upon the sea;
Yet oft I think the ocean they've sailed o'er
    Is deeper known upon the strand to me.
The middle sea contains no crimson dulse,
    Its deeper waves cast up no pearls to view;
Along the shore my hand is on its pulse,
    And I converse with many a shipwrecked crew.

—Henry David Thoreau

Mussel shells on beach, Double Beaches

Lichens on rock, grass, Little Spruce Head Island

> Age on age the rocks remain,
> And the tides return again;
> Only we poor mourners, sinners,
> Weavers, toilers, fishers, spinners,
> Pass away like visions of rain.
>
> —Gavin Maxwell

Eider duck nest, Barred Island

The eider ducks have arrived to breed about the shore and the islands; they bring with them that most evocative and haunting of all sounds....
—GAVIN MAXWELL

White flowers and rock, Barred Island

The great rhythms of nature, to-day so dully disregarded, wounded even, have here their spacious and primeval liberty; cloud and shadow of cloud, wind and tide, tremor of night and day. Journeying birds alight here and fly away again all unseen, schools of fish move beneath the waves, the surf flings its spray against the sun.

—Henry Beston

Beach dandelions, Little Spruce Head Island

Barred Island gull's nest

> I have been here before,
>   But when or how I cannot tell:
> I know the grass beyond the door,
>   The sweet keen smell,
> The sighing sound, the lights around the shore.
>
> —DANTE GABRIEL ROSSETTI

What can we salvage from the ocean's strife
More lovely than these skeletons that lie
Like scattered flowers open to the sky.
Yet not despoiled by their consent to life?

Crabs legs and shells, Great Spruce Head Island (South woods)

Bunchberries, North Point, Great Spruce Head Island

What a place to live, what a place to die, and be buried in. There certainly men would live forever, and laugh at death and the grave. There they could have no such thoughts as are associated with the village graveyard...

—Henry David Thoreau

These were the woods the river and sea
        Where a boy
    In the listening
Summertime of the dead whispered the truth of his joy
To the trees and the stones and the fish in the tide.
—Dylan Thomas

IN WOODS AND MEADOWS

And the azurous hung hills are his world-wielding shoulder
    Majestic—as a stallion stalwart, very-violet-sweet!—
These things, these things were here and but the beholder
    Wanting.
—Gerard Manley Hopkins

Bayberry and juniper and huckleberry begin at the very edge of the granite rim of shore, and where the land slopes upward from the bay in a wooded knoll the air becomes fragrant with spruce and balsam. Underfoot there is the multipatterned northern ground cover of blueberry, checkerberry, reindeer moss and bunchberry, and on a hillside of many spruces, with shaded ferny dells and rocky outcropping . . . there are lady's-slippers and wood lilies and the slender wands of clintonia with its deep blue berries.

—Rachel Carson

Sarsaparilla and spruces, Great Spruce Head Island

Bunchberry leaves, North Point, Great Spruce Head Island

I could scrape the colour
  from the petals,
like spilt dye from a rock
  —H.D. (Hilda Doolittle)

Yellow grass, North Meadow, Great Spruce Head Island

... Of all the everyday plants of this earth, grass is the least pretentious and the most important to mankind. It clothes the earth in an unmistakable way. Grass is simplicity itself. Not the simplicity of the uncomplicated unicellular life of stagnant water, but specialized simplicity unmatched in the fields. All the grasses, even the corn and wheat and barley and oats, have achieved a kind of perfection by eliminating nonessentials. Their stems are seldom branched.

Blue berries and lichens, North Meadow, Great Spruce Head Island

Their leaves need no stem of their own, and they are long, tapering, economical expanses of chlorophyll. Their flowers have dispensed with petals, scent and honey, since they need neither bee nor butterfly to pollinate them. The wind does that job.

So there it is, the simple grass, perfect for its purpose and found almost everywhere that plants can grow. —Hal Borland

Raspberry leaves, North Meadow, Great Spruce Head Island

> No white nor red was ever seen
> So am'rous as this lovely green.
> Annihilating all that's made
> To a green thought in a green shade.
> —Andrew Marvell

Lo! in the middle of the wood,
The folded leaf is wooed from out the bud....
With winds upon the branch, and there
Grows green and broad, and takes no care
Sun-steeped at noon.
—Alfred Tennyson

Skunk cabbage, Great Spruce Head Island

I like trees because they seem more resigned
to the way they have to live than other things do.
—Willa Cather

FOREST DETAIL

The economy of nature, its checks and balances, its measurements of competing life —all this is its great marvel and has an ethic of its own.
—Henry Beston

Cobwebs on grass, Great Spruce Head Island

And the white dew on the new bladed grass
Just piercing the dark earth, hung silently.
—Percy B. Shelley

I see a chaos of green leaves and fruit
Built round dark caverns, even to the root
Of the living stems that feed them — in whose bowers
There sleep in their dark dew the folded flowers.
—Percy B. Shelley

Fungus and grass, Great Spruce Head Island

Spruce trees in fog, Great Spruce Head Island

How still it is here in the woods. The trees
Stand motionless, as if they do not dare
To stir, lest it should break the spell. The air
Hangs quiet as spaces in a marble frieze.
—Archibald Lampman

Blue lichens, Great Spruce Head Island

> The blue's but a mist from the breath of the wind,
> A tarnish that goes at the touch of the hand.
> —Robert Frost

Lower branches of spruce, Great Spruce Head Island

What is the value of preserving and strengthening this sense of awe and wonder, this recognition of something beyond the boundaries of human existence? . . . Those who contemplate the beauty of the earth find reserves of strength that will endure as long as life lasts. There is symbolic as well as actual beauty in the migration of the birds, the ebb and flow of the tides, the folded bud ready for the spring. There is something infinitely healing in the repeated refrains of nature—the assurance that dawn comes after night, and spring after the winter.

—Rachel Carson

Black-throated Green Warblers, Great Spruce Head Island

Small balsam, Great Spruce Head Island

A rainy day is the perfect time for a walk in the woods.... always thought so myself; the Maine woods never seem so fresh and alive as in wet weather. Then all the needles on the evergreens wear a sheath of silver...

—RACHEL CARSON

Ferns, Great Spruce Head Island

Ferns seem to have grown to almost tropical lushness and every leaf has its edging of crystal drops. .

White-throated Sparrow, Great Spruce Head Island

Then the song of a whitethroat, pure and ethereal, with the dreamy quality of remembered joy...

—Rachel Carson

Strangely colored fungi —mustard-yellow and apricot and scarlet —pushing out of the leaf mold and all the lichens and the mosses have come alive with green and silver freshness.

—Rachel Carson

Tree trunk and fungus, Great Spruce Head Island

It looks as though, as a part of nature, we have become a disease of nature —
perhaps a fatal disease. And when the host dies, so does the pathogen. . . .
[Insofar as man's relations with the rest of nature are concerned,] I think we
must make every effort to maintain diversity —that we must make this effort
even though it requires constant compromise with apparent immediate needs.

—Marston Bates

LIFE CYCLES

> There is a place of trees . . . gray with lichen.
> I have walked there
>   thinking of old days.
> —Ezra Pound

Lichen and birch bark, Great Spruce Head Island

. . . ever pushing the boughs of the fir and spruce aside . . . contending day and night, night and day, with the shaggy demon vegetation, travelling through the mossy graveyard of trees.

—HENRY DAVID THOREAU

Dead tree, Great Spruce Head Island

Sure thou didst flourish once! and many springs,
Many bright mornings, much dew, many showers,
Pass'd o'er thy head; many light hearts and wings,
Which now are dead, lodg'd in thy living bowers.
   —HENRY VAUGHAN

Cobwebs and raindrops, Great Spruce Head Island

Hermit Thrush nest, Great Spruce Head Island

Star flowers, Great Spruce Head Island

This forest was not gloomy. It gave one the sense of life. Often old trees would be spaced as much as twenty feet apart. . . . In the heat of midday a faint perfume of balsam enriched the air. Now and then with the winding of the path we became conscious of the sea murmuring quietly along the outer edge of the trees as they descended to the shore.

—CHARLES CHILD

Moss, lichen, decayed wood, Great Spruce Head Island

. . . living green logs, hanging with moss and lichen, and with the curls and fringes of the yellow-birch bark, and dripping with resin, fresh and moist, and redolent of swampy odors, with that sort of vigor and perennialness even about them that toadstools suggest.

—Henry David Thoreau

There is wind in the tree, and the
    gray ocean's
Music on the rock.
                    —Robinson Jeffers

BY THE SEA WIND

In defying nature, in destroying nature, in building an arrogantly selfish, man-centered, artificial world, I do not see how man can gain peace or freedom or joy. I have faith in man's future, faith in the possibilities latent in the human experiment: but it is faith in man as a part of nature, working with the forces that govern the forests and the seas; faith in man sharing life, not destroying it.

—Marston Bates

Old spruce and young spruces, Great Spruce Head Island

It is not their bones or hide or tallow that I love most. It is the living spirit of the tree, not its spirit of turpentine, with which I sympathize, and which heals my cuts. It is as immortal as I am . . .

—Henry David Thoreau

Parula Warbler, Great Spruce Head Island

We need another and a wiser and perhaps a more mystical concept of animals. Remote from universal nature, and living by complicated artifice, man in civilization surveys the creature through the glass of his knowledge and sees thereby a feather magnified and the whole image in distortion. We patronize them for their incompleteness, for their tragic fate of having taken form so far below ourselves. And therein we err, and greatly err. For the animal shall not be measured by man. In a world older and more complete than ours they move finished and complete, gifted with extensions of the senses we have lost or never attained, living by voices we shall never hear. They are not brethren, they are not underlings; they are other nations, caught with ourselves in the net of life and time, fellow prisoners of the splendour and travail of the earth.

—Henry Beston

Lichen-covered trees, Double Beaches, Great Spruce Head Island

Whatever attitude to human existence you fashion for yourself, know that it is valid only if it be the shadow of an attitude to Nature. A human life, so often likened to a spectacle upon a stage, is more justly a ritual. The ancient values of dignity, beauty, and poetry which sustain it are of Nature's inspirration; they are born of the mystery and beauty of the world. Do no dishonour to the earth lest you dishonour the spirit of man. Hold your hands out over the earth as over a flame. To all who love her, who open to her the doors of their veins, she gives of her strength, sustaining them with her own measureless tremor of dark life. Touch the earth, love the earth, honour the earth, her plains, her valleys, her hills, and her seas; rest your spirit in her solitary places. For the gifts of life are the earth's and they are given to all, and they are the songs of birds at daybreak, Orion and the Bear, and dawn seen over ocean from the beach.

—Henry Beston

Beach goldenrod, Great Spruce Head Island

Shore in fog, Great Spruce Head Island

. . . one's first appreciation is a sense that the creation is still going on, that the creative forces are as great and as active today as they have ever been, and that to-morrow's morning will be as heroic as any of the world. *Creation is here and now.* So near is man to the creative pageant, so much a part is he of the endless and incredible experiment, that any glimpse he may have will be but the revelation of a moment, a solitary note heard in a symphony thundering through debatable existences of time. Poetry is as necessary to comprehension as science. It is impossible to live without reverence as it is without joy.

—Henry Beston

Lichens on rocks, Barred Island

A natural discipline and intrinsic rhythm establishes itself, free from the strains and tensions of clock-watching. You have a sense of abiding by broad universal laws rather than of being bound by narrow and arbitrary rules. You feel free of bondage and yet secure in an order that governs the rest of the world around you—the march of fogs from the sea, the mating of foxes in the spring, the migration of birds in the fall. The pendulum of the clock has nothing to do with you, nor have its sweeping hands. Only the great pendulum of the tide can drive you away from the sand bar where you have been gathering blue mussels; only the slow hand of the declining sun can call you home from mulberry-picking on the heath. You experience the sense of well-being that comes from complete harmony with your surroundings, and you find it good.

—Louise Dickinson Rich

Seaweed in water, Little Spruce Head Island

Who will remember, who will know again
That isolate island in sight of the mainland?
The long cough of the rocky beach, the rusty pools
Where small crabs hustled green into darker weeds?
Who will study the subterranean pockets
Tough-walled with mussels and periwinkle blue
In the flashes of light on the iodine-odored sea?
Who will know what it is in the summer noon
To stand and look back at the continental shore
As far on the harbor as if it were forever?
Who will remember how it is to kneel
By the pink and purple beach peas,while the salt
Wind bends over filled with a wild-rose drench?
Or stare from the ridge at the whole island's length
Bow to stern in one embracing glance?
Who else would hear voices that are not there
Where we gazed up at tall and talking people?
On the treeless ridge in grass knee-high?
Who will know again? Who will remember
As children in the sun who loved that island?

—Winfield Townley Scott

Double Beaches in fog, Great Spruce Head Island

Push not off from that isle; thou canst never return.
—Herman Melville